COP TALK

COP TALK

A Dictionary of Police Slang

Aaron C. and Lewis J. Poteet

Writers Club Press
San Jose New York Lincoln Shanghai

Cop Talk
A dictionary of police slang

Writers Club Press
an imprint of iUniverse.com, Inc.

For information address:
iUniverse.com, Inc.
620 North 48th Street, Suite 201
Lincoln, NE 68504-3467
www.iuniverse.com

ISBN: 0-595-13375-4

Printed in the United States of America

PREFACE

This book was born out of my lifelong fascination with police, crime, and justice and my father's love of language, which he passed on to me. Much like the first book we co-authored, *Hockey Talk*, its genesis occurred as a byproduct of my work/play in the field. The power of the spoken word is nowhere more evident than in the world of law enforcement. A cop needs to understand what's being said on the street and then use the right words to resolve the situation as peacefully as possible. Words also play an important part in stress reduction for cops: a pretty healthy way to deal with stress and unpleasant things you can't change is by joking about them. The rollercoaster ride of terror and boredom that is a police officer's lot in life, demands a release, so not surprisingly *Cop Talk* is full of gallows humor. There is a whole lot of hurry-up-and-wait in police work, so "shooting the shit", "busting each others balls", and wisecracking are major time passers. Maybe that's why there's so much great police slang out there.

The Decision to Serve

My decision to pursue a career in law enforcement surprised my friends and family, since I was such a wild one as a child. I was always getting into trouble at school, I didn't respect authority, and my actions were not always on the right side of the law. But I didn't have any problem with this seeming contradiction myself. If anything, my wild roots helped prepare me for dealing with the criminal element better. I could see their side better and that helped me when relating to them. I switched sides because I wanted to be the hero not the villain, do the right thing. But I still wanted to be involved in the action. I was drawn to the excitement. Aren't we all? Look at the schoolyard fight that draws a crowd, the lure of the highway accident causing **rubber necking** or **turkey-necking** amongst passersby, the popularity of crime and police TV shows and movies. In America, crime and crimefighters are a national obsession.

Even though I spent much of my youth in supposedly crime-free Canada, somehow I still developed a taste for the street. At first trouble just seemed to find me; later on I would seek it out. My family traveled quite a bit while I was growing up and this was an education of sorts for me. During our travels I set out on my own a lot, roaming around the streets of Montreal and cities across the United States and Mexico by myself even before my teens, hitchhiking, getting into fights, inadvertently making myself an ideal victim for predatory street crime. Not surprisingly, I was mugged a couple of times in Montreal and Boston, had my wallet pickpocketed in Mexico, chased and threatened in various US cities., etc. It wasn't a boring childhood.

I remember one time in particular, when I was about twelve, I was walking through a mall in downtown Montreal, when this big street tough just latched on to me, making threats, demanding money (the street term for this activity is **taxing**). I broke free and ran, but he caught me just outside the mall. There was a man standing at the bus stop whom I asked for help. The hood was a foot taller than me with a big fat dark-haired head and looked nothing like me, but he told the man he was my older brother. "He's my brudda," he said. The man at the bus stop seemed to decide to believe it so he didn't have to get involved. Then I saw a man in uniform maybe two hundred feet down the street. I yelled and ran towards him, and the hood fled back into the mall. After I spoke with the cop briefly, I confronted Mr. John Q. Public bystander at the bus stop: he wouldn't even look me in the face. I realized that even though he was a foot taller than the street punk, he was scared of him. I decided that there were two types of people: those that avoided trouble (like the chickenshit at the bus stop) and those that faced trouble head-on, sought it out (like the policeman who helped me). I resolved to be one of the latter.

During my 'twenties, I lived and died (or at least took a few pretty bad beatings) by my resolution not to back down from trouble. Soon I learned you had to choose your battles carefully. I used to cut through Roxbury (a Boston ghetto) as a shortcut home after work until one time I had to throw one kid into a wall and then run from his rock-throwing colleagues to escape. Another time I intervened when a lunatic was harassing people on a subway platform. A violent struggle ensued, in which I was almost knocked unconscious from a blow to the head. As a train approached, I gained the upper hand and nearly threw my assailant onto the tracks in front of the oncoming train. These and other incidents helped me to learn the longer but more peaceful path of least resistance. I began to see the value of talking your way through a problem.

Although my upbringing was far from ideal, I feel that my parents instilled in me good values and a sense of fairplay and honor. Once I began to see how unjust the real world could be, it bothered me. I think it was this disillusionment with the sorry world we live in, which sent me in the direction of law enforcement. (That and not wanting to work in an office job.) As I became older and more able to defend myself and others, I set out to even the score. First I was a Guardian Angel and in a neighbourhood patrol group called StreetSafe; later I worked as a Special Police Officer in downtown Boston for the better part of a decade. As an SPO (basically a glorified security guard with arrest powers) in a high crime area, I learned many things about the street. The job was an ideal training ground for law enforcement officers. We used to joke that there was some kind of force of nature or gravitational pull that drew crazy, fucked-up people to our "property." We made hundreds of arrests each year, but our goal was always to try to resolve the problems without force or too many unnecessary arrests. In 1992 I moved to Texas and served briefly with the Austin Police Force. Despite all the aggravation, double shifts, and mountains of paperwork, I enjoyed my time in law enforcement. I found out I wasn't a superhero. But I had my moments. When I think back on my years of service, I remember times I made a difference, helped people out, and/or took a reckless person off the streets (if only temporarily). But I only dabbled in law enforcement compared to some. My hat is off to all those who serve honestly. They deserve a raise!

To Serve And Protect

Writing about police and the nature of police work is a walk through a tired cliché minefield. I'll try to be brief. Sure, being a cop can be a thankless, depressing, heart-hardening experience—this point is underscored by the high divorce and suicide rates (see **swallowed the .38 caliber aspirin**) found among those that work in law enforcement. Seeing more than your share of the dark side of human nature can make a person bitter and mistrustful of other people (see **asshole theory**). As a cop you often catch people on their worst day (see **double whammy**), if you are lucky (or good) you catch them midway through committing a shameful, violent, or very embarrassing act. Even the people you're trying to help often aren't that happy to see you, especially if the damage is already done (as it so often is). "It's about time you got here. I guess we shoulda called Dunkin Donuts instead of 911"!

All this and the so-called revolving doors of the judicial system make a cop's work seem pointless and frustrating at times. The bottom line is that the job breeds cynicism. Talk to any cop who has been on the job for a while, and I can assure you of finding one of two things: someone who has become cynical and negative or someone who has learned to cope with the negativity and harsh reality he has had to face day in and day out on the job.

Working the street you see some crazy and horrible things. I've seen a mother use her baby to help her shoplift. I've seen kids practice Karate kicks on an elderly homeless man. I've seen plenty of 'unhappy campers', victims of various crimes. I've seen hundreds of fights, hundreds of 'sucker punches'. One time I had to break up a fight in which one of the combatants tried to bite the other's ear off (this was pre-Tyson/Holyfield fight). They had started out trading punches, then came together wrestling each other to the ground. Rolling around on the ground, one of them bit into the others ear, locked his jaw and wouldn't release it. By the time we arrived on the scene, there was a crowd standing around speculating on whether the ear was going to come all the way off or not. As we tried to break up the fight, we couldn't get the guy to release his crocodile bite on this poor guy's ear. We're yelling and poking him in the ribs, finally I jammed my thumb hard into his cheek up at the top of the jawbone to force his jaw open. The kid's ear was 'dogmeat' by the time we got it free. (For more stories see appendix 2).

The Job really brought home the reality that boredom was the great enemy. I used to get so bored, I welcomed the fight calls, the crimes in progress, the crazy situations as a break in the monotony. It was a great lesson in perspective shifting. One minute you're hoping something will happen to make your shift pass quickly. Anything; an alarm, a 'cat fight', a 'domestic'… Next minute you're rolling around on the ground, fighting for your life with some lunatic, wishing it had been a quiet night after all.

If the job is so awful, what makes it so appealing to those who get the "calling"? Those of us that have worked the street love "the job," as it is affectionately referred to. It's more than a job; it's a way of life, and many times you hear cops exclaim: "Can you believe I get paid to do this?" Much like being a preacher or being in the military, people that work in law enforcement are drawn to this work, and have little desire to do anything else, despite low pay, long hours, and adverse working conditions. Is it the excitement? The camaraderie? The pride in standing up for what is right? (See **thin blue line**).

Whatever naïve idealistic misconceptions a police recruit might have gone into the job with, he stays because he likes the work, the thrill, the variety, the life. I'm here to tell you that the adrenaline that fills you during a foot chase, breaking up a big fight, or making a felony arrest is addictive. This passion is reflected in the slang, and for cops talking about the job is a thrill because they love what they do.

So why such colorful speech? Maybe the secret lies in the old expression: "The Job is 90% boredom and 10% sheer terror". It makes for a lotta time to shoot the shit! Where I worked we spent lots of that would-be boring time, telling and retelling colorful street or criminal encounters we'd experienced. This helped pass the time, and the 'war stories" got better with each telling. Talking and joking, making light of some of the more terrifying, depressing, or disgusting episodes that occurred (in the 10% sheer terror time) was a sort of therapy for us, I guess —an attempt to come to terms with and move on from memories that might otherwise haunt us. So using an expression like **"doing the funky chicken"** to describe some poor bastard's last movements may seem cold, but, well.... It's making light of a harsh reality —one the cops didn't create, but are always called on to clean up. OK, maybe mostly we talked, joked, to pass the time and just have some fun.

But gallows humor aside, words and slang play an important role in a policeman's day-to-day work because cops use them to function efficiently on the street. Cops need to know all the slang around so they understand what's going on. Drug lingo, black speak, hustler hype, mafia terms, prison culture, you name it...a cop survives by being able to figure out what's going on when he arrives at a situation and then using the appropriate combination of negotiation, intimidation, threat and (if all else fails) force. The ideal resolution to most police calls is that the officer finds the right words to resolve the situation without having to subdue or arrest anyone. In this way, a cop's skills with language become his most *often used* and *valuable* worktools.

So all this boils down to a very rich environment for slang and word play. The more creative the better, the more cynical the better, the more amusing the better, the more disgusting...all the better. A cop's world is uncensored and at times outrageous, and the words and phrases they use reflect that some of the stuff cops get caught up in just didn't have adequate words or expressions to describe them before cops invented them. So patrol officers use the word "**hinky**" to express the feeling that a person or situation just didn't seem to fit or feel right: "There was something 'hinky' about the guy....walking out of that grocery store with a bulky coat on a warm day looking around nervously" or "man my '**spider sense**' went off when that man came running out of the back door of that sorority house." (In fact, we found the word 'hinky' used to describe part of the process that led to the arrest of a Texas serial rapist.)

Observe NYPD detectives of the 75 (precinct) as they visit the ER with a shooting victim and a "**green**" (read *new*) detective:

Next to the victim a nurse was greasing the end of a catheter. With the catheter in her right hand, the nurse grabbed the man's penis with her left and used her first right finger and thumb to separate the lips on the organ's head.......

....Smitty saw the look on Dave's face and guffawed. "In the squad, this is what we call the **Johnson Tube Sit-up Test**," he said. "She's going to shove that tube up his Johnson, right? If the guy bolts up or screams, it means he feels it and he's going to live. If there's no reaction, then it's the pearly gates for him. Or maybe purgatory."

Veteran detectives knew this procedure was part of the medical management of shock when a person suffered a major trauma such as a motor vehicle accident or gunshot wound. Massive blood loss was rapidly remedied with fluids, but because of the risk of overloading the heart and lungs with fluid, a catheter was introduced directly into the bladder to measure urine output precisely so doctors could meet the body's fluid demand properly. But it looked like some insanely barbaric method of torture to Dave....

"Doctors say there's no medical basis to the **Johnson Tube Sit-up Test**," Smitty continued, thoroughly enjoying the sick expression on Dave's face. "But we've found that ninety percent of the time we can use it to predict whether someone will live or die. We know whether to stick around and interview the victim or not."

Dave continued to stare at the man, pondering the excruciating notion of having a long rubber tube ramrodded into one's schlong.

—from *The Making of a Detective*, by Harvey Rachlin (Dell, 1995).

Other phrases came out of the need for more colorful or concise expressions to describe things. I like the different slang names for various crimes:

carjacking—robbery of vehicle
chew and screw—eat at restaurant and leave without paying
cowtipping—cruelty to animals?
drive-by—shoot people from moving car
hacking—computer fraud
mailbox baseball—juvenile vandalism game
push-in robbery—robber catches victim at his door, and pushes him inside to rob.

And so on…The list of crazy crimes with cool nicknames is endless. So sit back and enjoy the words of the street. And please don't blame us if they offend you. Remember, many cops had to live and die through the stuff that created these expressions. Oh, and if you know of any offensive or inoffensive but colorful words and phrases we may have missed, please send them to us at *lpoteet@info-internet.net* or *apoteet@austin.rr.com*.

Aaron C. Poteet, Austin TX June 2000

COP TALK

A Dictionary of Police Slang

*—"the inventive and often scatological jargon common to cops"—John Haslett Cuff, "What's a nice guy doing in a precinct like this," Toronto **Globe and Mail** (November 21, 1994).*

accelerant—gasoline or other highly flammable liquid used to accelerate spread of fire by arsonist. Technical jargon among arson investigation officers. Fletcher, *Pure Cop,* p. 53. See also **pour patterns, burn patterns.**

accidentally on purpose—jocular, sarcastic oxymoronic reference to a murder, attempted murder, or other crime made to look like an accident. "Just as he stepped off the curb, he was killed by a passing car, accidentally on purpose."—De Sola, p. 2.

acid—LSD, LSD-25, Lysergic acid diethyalamide, "Chief." Psychoactive drug with strong hallucinatory effects, popularized in the 1960s. See **Blue Acid.**

acidhead—habitual user of LSD. Also known as **a cubehead.**

Adam Henry—code from the police phonetic alphabet for "asshole." "Hey, Sarge, why can't I book him? He's a real **Adam Henry**."—"L.A. Speak," *Los Angeles Times Magazine*, March 26, 1995.

aggravated assault—assault with a deadly weapon, one that causes serious bodily injury or one that is committed against a police officer. The most ingenious in-your-face explanation of one of these charges was the soul singer James Brown's, who was charged with committing it: "I aggravated them [the police] and they assaulted me." He was convicted anyway.

airmail—"concrete, bricks, and the like hurled down from rooftops onto patrol cars responding to a call."—Philbin, p. 2. See also **nair bomb, flaming shit bomb, Carolina pancake.**

alien sting—"British police recently broadcast an emergency message to patrolling officers, warning that a flying saucer had crashed and burned in Appleton, Cheshire, and that the area was radioactive. Five civilians who showed up were arrested. The police had copied this 'alien sting' idea from a U. S. magazine, hoping to nab snoopers who listen illegally to their communications."—from "Word Watch," in "Social Studies" column in early 1993 Toronto *Globe and Mail.*

A L J—"acting like a jerk," not an offense in any of the criminal codes, but expressive of one of the reasons other than overt criminal activity that can attract the unfavorable notice of the police; that is to say, an **enforcement rationale**, not a charge. "Why'd you bring him in?" "Oh, I booked him on ALJ alone." From David M. Boatright, instructor, Texas Peace Officer Laws class, Austin TX Community College, 1993. This set of letters, this acronym, is one of several which are police slang parodies of such standard terms as **DWI, DUI** ("Driving While Intoxicated," "Driving Under the Influence.") See also "arrested him **on looks alone,**" **attitude arrest**, "being an **asshole in the nighttime.**"

alley apple—rock or brick used in street fight. Nash

alligatoring—type of burn pattern on wood, evidence to an arson investigator. "When wood burns, it looks like an alligator's back when it's completely burnt away. The depth of the alligator char will tell you how long this particular piece of wood was burning. The color of the alligatoring will tell you if any accelerant was used."—Fletcher, *Pure Cop*, p. 54.

alphabet soup—a reference to the jumble of organizations that can become involved in a case—the DEA, CIA, FBI, ATF, etc.

ambulance chaser—lawyer, insurance salesman, or anyone who follows ambulances to benefit off other people's misfortunes. See also **turkey necker.**

amyl nitrate—inhalant speed-like drug. See **poppers.**

AMP—"amputated," used to explain missing entries on police fingerprint forms.—Special Fraud Squad glossary of abbreviations and jargon, New York City. See **MAB.**

amphetamine—speed, stimulant drug, increases activity of central nervous system.

angel dust—synthetic drug used as a horse tranquilizer, which tends to make human users violent and dangerous. Also called PCP, Horse, "PCP on Parsley" or Killer weed.

anything you say will be held against you—probably more than one lippy suspect has responded to this part of the standard arrest warning with "Your wife's big breasts!"

A P B—All Points Bulletin, also known as a **citywide.** See also **BOLO.**

arm on—to ask for financial help, as one (ex)officer, out of work and down on his luck, to another. "I'm not looking to arm on to anybody."— NYPD Blue.

arsenal—supply of weapons or drugs.

artillery—equipment of destruction: equipment for injecting drugs—the **works,** the needle, eyedropper, spoon, bottle cap, cotton and cloth, string, or belt for a tourniquet.

Aryan Brotherhood—Neo-Nazi white supremacist prison/street gang alleged to be involved in contract killings.—De Sola.

assassin's special—22 calibre automatic weapon with a silencer, a favorite weapon of Mafia killers.—De Sola, Nash arrested him for being an **asshole in the nighttime**—variation on criminal law breaking and entering in the nighttime. "What am I being arrested for?" "For being an asshole [or dickhead] in the nighttime!" See also **ALJ, DWHUH, attitude arrest.**

ass-kisser—person who sucks up to boss(es) or anyone in authority. **bootlicker, brownnoser.**

assallant—according to one observer, a word used in stereotypical ways, as, for example, for a "black guy running north or in California, a hispanic guy running east."—see **perpetrator.**

asshole theory—widely held by veteran policemen, it starts with the belief, when you begin, that there are a few assholes out there, and you need to watch out for them. Soon, you begin to think everyone but cops are assholes; then it's everyone except your shift; then it's everyone but your partner, and sometimes you wonder about him.—Dean Thompson, SWAT team sergeant, DFW Airport.

at-risk youth—new euphemism for "juvenile delinquent," this phrase refers to youth who are put in a home because they're "at risk" of getting in trouble with the law. Similar, but not the same, is a Texas acronym, **CHINS,** "child in need of supervision," to designate young people not yet officially delinquent but exhibiting behaviors marginally tending or leading toward a life of crime. e.g. truancy, running away from home. Etc,

attitude adjustment—change someone's attitude with a beating. One of the goals of doing a **Rodney King** on a suspect. "He looks like he needs an attitude adjustment," the cop says, patting his nightstick.

attitude arrest—arrest made because a police officer does not like someone's attitude or behavior. Shouldn't happen by itself, as arrests are legally authorized only on "probable cause", when officer has reason to believe an offense has been committed. But see **ride, contempt of cop, ALJ.** From

David M. Boatright, instructor, Texas Peace Officer Laws class, Austin TX Community College, 1993.

auto banalisé—unmarked police car, especially a compact, in Québec French. "Police call them 'autos banalisées...cars that look plain or banal."—Montréal *Gazette*, October 17, 1993. A "plain Jane" (*Car & Motorcycle Slang*).

baby bear—a police trainee or rookie.—De Sola.

bacon—as in "I smell bacon," common street response to police arrival on the scene. From the 60s insult: policemen were sometimes called **pigs**. The countervailing image is captured in "the city's Finest," cops as elite, above average citizens, the **thin blue line.**

backtracking—reconstructing what victims were doing before event.

back up—provide physical assistance. "Officer in trouble at Oak and Main. I need back up now." Also refers to verbal support: "Sergeant, if you don't believe me, ask O'Malley. He'll back me up on this" (i. e. tell the same story). "He wouldn't back up his own mother." See **stand-up guy.**

badge—male cops' oral rule: be careful: "Your badge will get you pussy, but the pussy will get your badge."—from Austin TX police department's warning to police cadets.

badge-heavy—adjective describing a police officer who revels in the power. **John Wayne syndrome.** Especially when found in a recruit, a real problem, but a source of trouble anywhere, anytime.

badge on a beaver—"female officer." (truckers talk)—Roth, *The Writer's Complete Crime Reference Book.*

the **bag**—the uniform. "I'm putting the bag back on for the uniform detail parade."—NYPD Blue. Northeastern U.S.

baghead—glue sniffer.

bag man—the person designated to collect, transport, and deliver cash, whether for criminal purposes, bribery, or political payoff. To be distinguished from **bag lady**, of course, who is a street person, homeless, who lives out of a bag, scrounges through garbage for anything of value, food, etc.

Fed

bail, bail out—suspects stop stolen vehicle being chased by police, jump out and take off on foot in different directions.

bait money—currency of which serial numbers and related information such as denominations have been prerecorded, to hand over in a robbery, to assist in tracing for conviction.

B & E—break and enter, also known as a "beanie." A burglary.

ballistics blanket—Kevlar bomb-blanket, used e.g. to cover a car moved in close to a situation, to stop bullets; or of course to cover a suspected bomb. **Bomb blanket.** Fletcher, *Pure Cop*, p. 260.

balls to spare—said of someone very brave, or foolish. Also **brass balls, stones, huevos, bucket of balls.** Guts, courage. Terrence E. Poppa, *Drug Lord*, p. 102. The opposite of **b-b balls** (someone with no courage).

Baltimore Korean corner store owner's robbery suspect identification credo—"All rook arike." Simon, *Homicide*, p. 414.

banging—throwing a stun grenade, in an assault or just before.

banker—street slang for the person who receives and holds cash paid out for drugs.—Stroud, *Close Pursuit*, p. 328.

barbiturates—drugs which depress the central nervous system. Also known as **downers.**

Barney Fife—a small-town policeman, with the image of a goofy little inept person with a badge. From the Andy Griffith show, a longtime source of police stereotypes from America's legendary sleepy-town self-image. See also **Bubba Fife, Mayberry police department.**

base—cocaine which has had hydrochloride removed. Also see **freebase.**

basehead—a cocaine user who **cooks freebase.**

baseball bat therapy—another way to say "beating some sense into somebody", one major way to accomplish **attitude adjustment** using a baseball bat.

Batman and Robin—"two officers in a patrol car." (trucker's slang)—Roth, *The Writer's Complete Crime Reference Book.*

batting practice—beating up a suspect with nightsticks.

he really does know **where the bear shit in the buckwheat**—said of a fellow criminal by another, their having just met and his having wondered whether the new partner may be all talk and no action, or dumb.—from Joseph Wambaugh's *The Onion Field.*

beat—an officer's area of responsibility for surveillance or patrol.

To "walk the beat" is to patrol.

beat down—ghetto, gang expression for particularly bad beating in street fight.

beat him like a dog—to use excessive force in handling a suspect. Also known as **pull an L. A., Rodney King him.**

beef—1. "issuance of a misconduct complaint...initiated by the public or the department. 'I can't believe I got **beefed** after that bust. What's the department coming to?'"—"L. A. Speak," *Los Angeles Times Magazine,* March 26, 1995.

    2. a fight or dispute that results in a police response.

    3. a problem between an officer and a suspect.

    4. "a specific criminal charge: 'what's the beef? suspect might ask detective. "Murder One" might be the response. =--Philbin, p. 2.

beer muscles—someone who has these is prone to fight due to alcohol consumption. See **liquid courage.**

Beilby's ball—An old reference to execution, from 18th and early 19th century England: "He will dance at Beilby's ball, where the sheriff pays the music; he will be hanged."—Grose, *1811 Dictionary of the Vulgar Tongue.* See **steps and the string.** This old dictionary of popular and underworld slang, reprinted in our time, offers many such phrases; we cite it here to give a sense of the continuity of a cynical tone in such language as street slang, underworld slang, and cop talk.

bennies—benzedrine, a amphetamine.

a **Bernie**—"after Bernhard Goetz; any victim who might be armed and prepared to use the weapon."—Carsten Stroud, ***Close Pursuit,*** p. 328. Limited to East Coast usage. A person who looks weak and defenseless but is actually quite capable of turning the tables on the would-be mugger. Goetz shot four youths in the New York subway after deciding they were apparently going to mug him

best cop money can buy—cynical reference to police corruption. It has been observed that in midwestern and northeastern US police forces, corruption is more likely to be a problem than violence; in the US South and Southwest, violence is more likely to be a problem than corruption.

better to be tried by twelve than carried by six—police proverb providing rationale for shooting first and asking questions later.—Wambaugh, ***Lines and Shadows***, p. 246.

BFR—"big fucking rocks." In San Antonio the police have adopted this acronym to use whenever anyone throws rocks to damage property or break a window. "He BFR'd the place," or "they used BFRs." The reference is to an incident during a SWAT operation in which "a little old man had shot a 22 rifle from his apartment. The SWAT team kept him up all night by throwing big rocks into his apartment, to keep him awake. In the morning, when the team tried to enter, the little old man had stacked all the rocks up against the door so they couldn't enter through the door. This happened about fifteen years ago, and the apartment complex had used the rocks for landscaping and there were a countless number of them."—David "Mike" Logsdon.

big hats—"State police only." (trucker's slang)—Roth, ***The Writer's Complete Crime Reference Book.***

big house—prison. See also the **joint.**

billy club—police service baton, also called billy, baton, **nightstick.**

Billyland—white trash neighbourhood in South Baltimore. "A recognized geographic entity among Baltimore cops"...."natural habitat for the descendants of West Virginians and Virginians who left the coal mines and the mountains to man Baltimore's factories during the second world war. A true Billyboy not only comes from Billyland, but 'spent half his life drinking at the B&O Tavern and the other half shuffling back and forth from the Southern District Court for theft, disorderly conduct, resisting arrest.....etc.'" "Then to a Baltimore detective you are a Billyboy, a white-trash redneck, a city goat, a dead-brained cul-de-sac of heredity, spawned in the shallow end of a diminishing gene pool."—Simon, *Homicide*, pp. 398-399. The term "billy" obviously comes from "hillbilly," which in turn has been traced to the use of certain Scottish-border troops by King William of England, to maintain order among unruly rebellious Scots; because they were effective in this wild, unrestrained fighting, they were used to fight Indians in the border zones of the American colonies, and became the root stock of the settlers in the hills of West Virginia, etc.; hence they were known as "hillbillies." "His family tree has no branches," said of such persons, was a sly way of referring to incest and inbreeding.

bird dog—person who sets up targets for arrest (informer).

2. as an internal police word, a verb denoting setting up in a spot to watch closely, for example, a stop sign, or to follow someone closely, for surveillance.

bis, biscuit—a hand gun. See also **jammie.**—Susanna Moore, *In the Cut.* Also, an **oo-wop.**

got the **bitch**—slang for a three-time loser criminal in Texas, who has already been twice convicted of felonies, and who, upon a third conviction, is sentenced as an "habitual" felony offender. The minimum sentence is increased from five years to twenty-five years confinement, and the offender is said to have "got the bitch," from "ha-*bitual.*"—From David M. Boatright, instructor, Texas Peace Officer Laws class, Austin TX Community College, 1993.

black and white—"police patrol car." (truckers' slang)—Roth, *The Writer's Complete Crime Reference Book.*

black and white fever—1. when a person runs or turns and walks away quickly when they see a police cruiser.—Wambaugh, *The New Centurions.*
2. the phenomenon of traffic slowing to watch any diversion, an accident, or a parked police car, a problem in urban areas. "Just the presence of a CHP [California Highway Patrol] officer slows down traffic."—Richard Simon, "Fast Living All Part of L.A.'s Freeway Culture," *LA Times* (February 26, 1995).

black beauties—amphetamines.

black tar heroin—Mexican heroin, described as dark brown with a clay texture.—Terrence E. Poppa, *Drug Lord,* p. 36, 109. Also **tootsie roll, black gold, shriek.**—Stroud, *Close Pursuit,* p. 329.

blammo ammo—"rubber bullets that don't penetrate the skin," useful to bounty-hunters, who want to deliver the perpetrator intact if possible, to collect the bounty.—Patrice O'Shaughnessy, "Bounty hunting 1994: Rambo learns philosophy," Montréal *Gazette* (January 30, 1994).

blanket party—prison guard/inmate (Los Angeles and Canadian) term for an event in which an inmate is beaten but first covered with a blanket, so that he can't identify his attackers. Originally from military slang, where the practice was a means of internal discipline in a company to avoid "company punishment," where the errors of one brought down punishment on all. See also **sock-hop.**—Yates, *Line Screw.*

blasting—use of explosives to attack a safe. **Soup jobs.**

blitz rape—"an unexpected sexual assault committed by a stranger."—Philbin, p. 17. He claims it was coined by Ann Burgess and Lynda Holmstrom in studies of rape victims in the early 1970s at Beth Israel Hospital in Boston.

Blood Island—Sicily, which is reputedly controlled by La Cosa Nostra (the Mafia).

Bloods—Los Angeles street gang, also called "crip killers," from the name of the leading opposing gang.

blossoming, blossomers—overambitious officers bucking for promotion by **brownnosing, asskissing.**—Wambaugh, *The New Centurions.*

blow—cocaine.

blue acid, blue angelfish, blue babies, blue bells, blue caps, blue chair, blue cheer, blue dragon, blue jeans, blue microdot, blue mist, blue pyramids, blue Splash, blue water—types of **LSD.** – Nash.

blue angels, blue birds, blue clouds, blue devils, blue dolls, blue heavens, blue horse, blues—types of **barbiturates** (amytal and amobarbital). —Nash.

blueboy—"local or state police." (trucker's slang)—Roth, *The Writer's Complete Crime Reference Book.*

blue flu—"disease" first named in the l960s from an incident by NYPD, to protest the way they thought the city was treating them, but also used by LAPD police—up to half of them—who called in sick May 30,31, June 1, 1994, to protest lagging contract talks. See also **thin blue line, blue wall of silence.**

blue knight—policeman.

blue laws—laws regulating drinking, dancing or working on Sundays.

blue man—uniformed police officer. See also **Boys in Blue**

blue movie—adult pornographic movies.

blue pellets—Cyanide pellets.

blue room—police interrogation room, where the third degree is administered.

blue sky—street slang for heroin. Also **liquid sky.**—Stroud, *Close Pursuit,* p. 329.

blue wall of silence—a reference to the tradition that police stick together and do not inform on each other. The suggestion is clear that they will cover up illegal or improper police conduct.—Stroud, *Close Pursuit,* p. 236.

blunt—1. As in "the blunt," underworld slang for "the money."
2. In drug parlance, a joint of marijuana rolled in a tobacco leaf, originally a leaf from a "Phillies Blunt cigar," according to Tom Dalzell, *The Slang of Sin.* This cheap, fat cigar was ideal for the purpose.

blunt instrument—Tom Philbin identifies this familiar term as actually euphemistic, covering a variety of weapons of assault and murder. "If someone were hit on the head with a ballpeen hammer, police would [say] the attack was made by a 'blunt instrument,'" but frying pans, candelabras, and in one case, a frozen leg of lamb, have been identified (in the latter case, the instrument later cooked and served to the investigating detectives. Philbin, p. 20.

boat and oar—prostitute, used because it rhymes with whore. There's a whole series of these phrases used in the late nineteenth and early twentieth century by US criminals as codes? See also **fish and shrimp (pimp), frog and feather (leather), husband and wife (knife), moan and wail (jail).** Nash.

bobbies—policemen in England, from Sir Robert Peel. See **peelers, rozzers, Bow Street Runners.**

body cavity search—a complete search, for drugs or smuggled jewels, including mouth, anus, vagina.....

boiler room—"a bare-bones room with desk, chairs, and telephones from which **con men** sell all kinds of fraudulent items from stock and land to chimney cleaning."—Philbin, p. 21.

BOLO—be on the lookout for. See **APB**.

Bombs 'R' Us—bomb squad name for electronics stores like Radio Shack, because "Most electronic components that bombers use can be purchased at any electronics place. We call these places 'Bombs 'R' Us.' They're the bomber's paradise because everything you need to make a bomb is there."—Fletcher, *Pure Cop,* p. 20.

book—to arrest and file charges again someone.

book bomb—an explosive concealed in a closed book which detonates when opened. See **Car Trap**. Nash.

bookie—a taker of bets.

boost—to steal. In NYPD, specifically, to shoplift.

boost and shoot—from "boost," an old word for "steal," adapted to describe stealing to support a junkie's need for drugs.

booster—professional or commercial shoplifter who steals merchandise for resale, usually to support drug habit. Hence also **car booster,** "one who steals from parked cars."—Special Fraud Squad glossary of abbreviations and jargon, New York City.

booster bloomers, booster skirts—clothing constructed or altered to enable wearer to secrete large quantities of stolen merchandise in it for concealing and carrying it out.—*Criminal Investigation*, p. 491.

boots—a new policeman, in San Antonio TX police slang. Also **new boot.** The name comes from the fact that a new recruit is issued new boots. According to David M. Logsdon, "the senior policemen usually consider you a 'boot' for the first five years of service."

bounty hunter—private contractor who gets paid a lump sum to bring fugitives who have jumped bail back to face trial or sentence. Usually former law enforcement officer. Also applied to a police officer who makes a lot of arrests.

Bow Street Runners—antedating even **bobbies** as a term for police in England, because the police station headquarters was in Bow Street. See also **bobbies, rozzers, peelers.**

boyfriend-girlfriend thing—one-word noun, for a "romantic dispute that turns homicidal." NYPD>—Count, *Cop Talk.*

bread—money, cash, **green.**

breecher—a member of a **SWAT** team who breaks down the door. Also known as a **slammer.**—Dean Thompson, DFW Airport **SWAT** team sergeant.

breeching tool—a sawed-off shotgun, to blow off the hinges when a **SWAT** team breaks down a door.

to Brodie—to jump, usually from a building or a bridge, from a Mr. Brodie, who claimed to have jumped off the Brooklyn Bridge.—Susanna Moore, *In the Cut.*

broom—New York City Police Department term for "station house attendant."

brought extra beef—brought extra manpower, muscle. Expecting trouble.—from TV show Cops, in Pittsburgh.

brown—1. Mexican heroin, usually of lower quality than white heroin. 2. homosexual multiple intercourse, not necessarily consensual, done by inmates in prison to a new arrival, known as a **gymnasium punk:** "The other guys bend him over a workout bar and **brown** him."—Joseph Wambaugh's *The Onion Field.*

brownie—"traffic officer."—Carsten Stroud, *Close Pursuit*. **meter maid, green onion.**

Bubba Fife—generic term for a big redneck policeman, a variant on **Barney Fife,** an inept small-town policeman.

bubble gum machine—said of old style police squad cars, because of the shape of the lights. Obsolete? Nash.

Buddha stick—cigarette filled with marijuana. See **blunt.**

bug—a criminal with a complete lack of empathic feeling. In Michael Yates' *Line Screw*, a mentally ill prison inmate (prison guard slang). Also used to describe an arsonist or a pyromaniac.

bugs—electronic transmitters, used for eavesdropping, collecting information. They include **room transmitter** (a device hidden in target's room and monitored from a short distance away); **phone tap/wiretap** (a transmitter in telephone for monitoring conversations); **body bug** (transmitter secreted on informer or undercover officer to record interaction with criminal target) (see **wearing a wire**); **bumper beeper** (a.k.a. **vehicle locater**), "battery-powered transmitter with huge magnet that bonds it to the underside of the target vehicle and which sends directional signals to the chase car."—Parkhurst, p. 128; **spike mike** or **thru-wall device** (microphone embedded through a tiny hole on the other side of the wall—"can hear whispers through concrete"; **laser shotgun bug** (device for remote sensing of conversations).

bull—convict/criminal name for cops, prison guards. **Screw, turnkey.**

bull dyke—tough, manly lesbian.

bullet—"a one-year prison sentence." "He pleaded guilty to battery and got a **bullet**."—"L.A. Speak," *Los Angeles Times Magazine* (June 13, 1995).

bullet head—see **head shapes.**

bullpen—also known as **holding tank**, the common cell where prisoners held until arraigned and assigned to individual cells.

bumper beeper—a tiny radio transmitter attached unobtrusively to a vehicle to make it easy to follow.

bunboys—insulting reference to the goon bodyguards for a gangland boss. Perhaps implies homosexuality. Also **butt buddy**.

bunco squads—police units assigned to solve con game fraud schemes.

burking—"homicidal suffocation," according to Philbin. He explains, "Back when cadavers were casually bought for medical experimentation, they brought a good price, and in Edinburgh, Scotland, in 1829, a man named William Burke was quite good at supplying them....He murdered people to create his supply. He and a confederate would get the victim drunk, then Burke would sit on the victim's chest while his partner held the person's mouth and nose closed. Result: a cadaver with no marks of foul play."—p. 31.

burning—a form of safecracking: use of acetylene torch or thermal burning bar to do safe-breaking. See also **the rip, blasting, drilling, manipulation.**

burn patterns—"low burning, high burning, different patterns of degree of burning in wood might suggest use of accelerant" and thus provide evidence of arson.—Fletcher, *Pure Cop*, p. 53.

bus and a boss, a—an ambulance and a supervisor. From Jeffrey Toobin's "The Unasked Question," *New Yorker* (March 6, 2000, p. 44). After the notorious late 1990s police killing of unarmed suspect Diallo in New York City, when one of the cops realized how serious a mistake had been made, he yelled into the radio, "Gimme a bus and a boss!"

bust balls—tease, harangue, give a hard time to, beat up. "Don't bust my balls."

busted out—to have made arrests on all cases one is working on.

—Mark Earhart, DFW SWAT team (motorcycle).

put the **button on him**—Chicago way to say "**flash the tin,**" or show badge to identify yourself.

button man—1. Chicago cop. In Chicago, the **button** is the badge, just as it is the **tin** elsewhere, and the **potsy** in New York.—Stroud, *Close Pursuit*, p. 237.
   2. a Mob (Mafia) soldier.

buttslam bar—cop slang for a homosexual bar. Also known as a **fudge packer bar.**

buy-bust—undercover narcotics officers' strategy involving drug purchase followed by arrest.

B. Y. O. B. gag—form of employee theft by bartenders where they bring their own bottle of booze and sell from it in bar to supplement income.— Joseph Wambaugh, *Fugitive Nights,* p. 138.

by the book—doing the job right, following proper police procedures and rules. Often said of a **clean cop**—"oh, he's by the book; he doesn't cut any corners." See also **by the numbers.** "Cross your T's and dot your I's on this one."

by the numbers—doing an investigation arrest or report the right way, not cutting any corners. "This is an extremely sensitive case; we're going to have to do this one 'by the numbers,' or it could blow up in our faces."

By-the-hour-motel—motel that caters to prostitutes and their customers.

cadaver dog—a policeman or a police dog with a talent for finding corpses.—from "Annals of Crime: A Violent Act," *New Yorker*, June 15, 1992.

call girl—a prostitute.

canaries—in **SWAT team** operations, hostages, as distinguished from **eagles** (fellow officers), **crows** (hostage-takers), and **parrots** (persons of whose loyalty or reliability one is uncertain).

cancel his ticket—shoot or kill him.

candids—surveillance photographs of suspect.

candyman—drug dealer or money man. See also **sugar daddy.**

cannon—NYPD term for a pickpocket. Anon., "Police Cant......oh yes they can!" *Spring 3100* (October 1958). See also **dip.**

to **cap**—"to shoot," as in "bust a cap in his black ass."—Susanna Moore, *In the Cut.*

cap a hooker—to convince a hooker to work for him, said of a pimp. Perhaps from "capture."—McCarthy, *Vice Cop.*

capped, iced—shot

capo—boss of a crime family or his lieutenant.

Captain's mole—officer placed on squad to spy on fellow officers and report to captain.

car bomb—bomb rigged to detonate when car is operated.

card mechanic—con man skilled at cheating at cards.

carjacking—new urban crime in North America, the term derived from "hijacking," because the new cars can't be operated without, in some cases, the "smart key," which has coded information without which systems stay shut down. So the thief waits at stop lights, jumps into the car, pushes the driver out or over, and flees in the BMW, Nissan, Acura, etc. Often done at gun- or knife-point.

car-keyed—a deliberate act, performed casually while walking along, the car key drawn along side of the car's paint work, scratching a long line down the side of the car. "Someone 'keyed my Volvo."

Carolina pancake—"mixture of lye and Crisco or bacon grease blended together and used as a weapon."—Philbin, p, 38. "Fat and lye…they cook it up and then throw it on you. The lye will burn right through you. You mix the lye with grease and you can't wash it off."—Mark Baker, *Cops: Their Lives in their Own Words.*

carpet muncher—suspect who grovels, brown-noses, kisses ass.

carry-off—form of safe-breaking (used instead of other methods like **burning, blasting, drilling, the Pry, the Rip,** etc.—carry off and break into at leisure).

cartwheels—amphetamines.

case, to—observe an establishment to plan a robbery or other criminal enterprise.

case goes down—case is solved.

cat burglar—person who breaks into houses at night, when people are often home, asleep, and tries to steal without awakening them. **Creeper.**

catch—handle a case. See **catching bench.**

catch car—drug squad van (NYPD) used in making arrests in **observation sales.**

Catch Club—jocular, fictional club to which bailiffs and sheriff's officers belong.—Grose, *1811 Dictionary of the Vulgar Tongue.*

you **catch 'em, you clean 'em**—slang maxim meaning "if you arrest them, you do the paper work, take any injured to the hospital, etc.

the **Catching Bench**—where civilians wait to speak with detectives about their cases.—from NYPD Blue 04/12/94.

cat fight—widely used among police as shorthand for "a fight between two women," which can be surprisingly vicious and violent.

C. C.—"condition corrected," "when a drug dealer is killed. When a normal person is killed it is 'a murder.'" When a drug dealer is killed, it is a "good murder," or "condition corrected."—Susanna Moore, *In the Cut.*

cement overshoes—jocular way of referring to execution and body disposal in one quick move. Gang murder technique in which victim's feet are weighted down with cement; then he is thrown into ocean, lake, river. See **footbath**.

center mass—"the spot in the middle of a suspect's chest, at about the third button," according to the Philadelphia Inquirer Magazine. "Police are taught to aim for this spot when they shoot."

chain referral schemes—see **pyramid schemes, Ponzi schemes.**

character—(n.) a career criminal. (TX)

Charlestown Townies—A Townie, white trash punk from Boston's Charlestown neighbourhood (where Bunker Hill is located, a tough, working-class Irish-American neighbourhood with, some say, the highest per capita number of convicted felons in the country. Mostly petty criminals, Townies are known to Boston law enforcement people as gutless punks who double-, triple-, and quadruple-team people in street fights.

Charlie's Angel—"female officer." (trucker's slang).—Roth, *The Writer's Complete Crime Reference Book.* See also **badge on a beaver, Dickless Tracy, Jane Wayne syndrome, Dirty Harriet syndrome, Mama bear..**

chase paper—investigate someone through the paper trail they leave: bills, public documents, etc. Parkhurst, p.152

cheap education—a cop's description of the effect on a suspect of an arrest, a brief questioning, or being detained for a short time. Often used to say why the cop lets a suspect go though he knows or suspects strongly that a charge might be filed: "why should I give him a cheap education?," with the implication that because the suspect has been let go, he or she will not be cautious and will be well and truly caught and charged later. See **mopery.**

cherry—a new prisoner, an obvious reference to the homosexual rape of new inmates.

chicken—underage street hustler.

chickenhawk—pedophile, **pedo,** a person who preys on underage victims sexually.

chicken powder—amphetamine powder.

chill, chill out—relax, calm down, subdue.

China death—heroin containing strychnine or cyanide.

China white—high-grade heroin from Southeast Asia.

CHINS—see **at-risk youth.**

chipper—a person who makes recreational use of illegal drugs, not an addict. (TX)

chips—girl/boyfriend. See also **hide.** (TX).

chirp—"A signal by pickpocket to stall; let victim out of **frame.**" (NYPD)—Anon., "Police Cant......oh yes they can!" *Spring 3100* (October 1958).

choir practice—Joseph Wambaugh's word for a fairly common recreation of policemen in which they go out into an isolated area and get drunk, drive recklessly, shoot guns off at random...etc. See Wambaugh's *The Choir Boys.*

choke hold—method of immobilizing a resisting perpetrator, using pressure on the carotid artery. Also called **sleeper hold.** See **funky chicken.**

chop shop—a stolen car disassembly place. See Poteet and Poteet, *Car & Motorcycle Slang* (iUniverse, 2000). Also, a morgue, medical examiner's office.

C. I.—confidential informer.

circling the gutter—Los Angeles Police Department term for the situation when they arrive at a crime scene and find a victim who is dying.

a **citywide**—an all-points bulletin, or **A P B.**

civilian—cop slang for anyone who isn't a police officer.

clean—out of drugs, not using drugs.

clean cop—an honest policeman. See **by the book, by the numbers.**

clean gun—a weapon that is unregistered and therefore untraceable is "clean" to the criminal; to the cop, as a Chicago police captain points out, it refers to a properly registered gun, the opposite!

Club Fed—one of the infamous minimum security "country club" federal prisons used mainly for housing rich or famous white collar criminals. "....There are no walls or bars. The prison could be any set of regulation buildings, and the khaki-clad staff members gulp when a visitor asks about the swimming pool, tennis courts, and miniature golf courses."— Parkhurst, *True Detectives*, p. 299. See movie "Club Fed" (1991).

clusterfuck—case handled poorly and/or messed up by too many well meaning police. "Four-star departmental clusterfuck." Sort of like "too many cooks spoil the broth."

cocabola—"a police nightstick, from the wood from which it was once made."—Susanna Moore, *In the Cut.*

cocaine—potent stimulant drug obtained from the coca leaf, also known as nose candy, blow, 'caine, coke, rich man's poison, cola.

cocaine cowboys—persons with a flashy lifestyle fueled by potent stimulant drug and lots and lots of money. Parkhurst, p. 34

code I—said of a police car which is proceeding to the scene without lights or siren.

code II—said of a police car proceeding to scene with lights only.

code III—said of a police car proceeding to scene with lights and siren.

coke whore—a woman or man who performs sexual services in return for cocaine.

cold turkey—withdrawal from drugs without medication. Skin resembles cold plucked turkey.

collar—arrest. "That arrest was my collar until that Fed stole it from me." In New York, "mobsters say 'pinch' when cops say 'collar.'"—Count, *Cop Talk.* Some other synonyms: "grab 'em," "bag 'em," "pick 'em up," "nail 'em."

collars for dollars—officers making lots of arrests for the overtime in court (extra pay).—*Rough Justice.*

Colombian necktie—"First I cut your throat from ear to ear, then I put your tongue through the slit, and watch you squirm."—from *Running Scared.*

"Gave him a necktie."—Stroud, p. 102.

Columbian roulette—smuggling drugs by swallowing packets in Columbia and then excreting them in US. If a packet breaks the smuggler could die. Nash.

colors—gang insignia, clothes.

Combat Zone—infamous area of downtown Boston once riddled with adult entertainment, prostitution and crime.

computer hack, hacker—person who gains unauthorized access to supposedly secure computer systems.

computer virus—disorganizing, disruptive program introduced into a computer system by a **computer hack** or **hacker.**

con—convict, incarcerated person.

concrete ranger, country ranger—contrasting tags to distinguish the modern Texas Ranger from the traditional one: "Today's Texas Ranger is just as apt to be a 'concrete ranger' as a 'country ranger,' cruising the interstate freeways of Houston or Dallas to pursue leads about drug dealers, conceded Tom Burks, curator of the Texas Ranger Hall of Fame and Museum, a tourist attraction in Waco."—Sam Howe Verhovek, "Women Rangers: Struggle in a Macho Bastion," New York *Times* (August 27, 1995).

concussion grenade—very loud firecracker to produce loud noise, big flash, to disorient hostage-taker.

connection—drug dealer.

condom carriers—drug couriers who swallow condoms full of drugs to cross border.

con game—short for **confidence game,** a scheme to cheat a gullible person out of money by gaining their confidence and playing upon their desire to make money fast and by an illegal manoeuvre, the illegality being used to prevent them from complaining later to the police. Varieties include the "**pigeon drop,**" "bank examiner scheme," "tv and liquor scams," "home repair fraud," "Spanish charities," "we'll make you a star."—Swanson, *Criminal Investigation,* p. 494-496. See also **fast change scam, quick change scam.**

connected—short for "well connected," means "has Mafia ties," or other protection through political or other loyalties, affinities, influences. "Don't mess with him, he's connected."

co-pilot—chaperone for someone on an acid trip.

consent search—a search in which the suspect has indicated willingness for or is subtly tricked into agreeing to a search, rather than making the policeman obtain a court order.

containment officers—see **SWAT team.**

contempt of cop—**enforcement rationale** or reason for a cop to investigate or give a suspect a hard time, modeled on the judges' "contempt of court." There's no such thing as "contempt of cop" in the law—you can't, theoretically, arrest someone for "contempt of cop," only for PC (probable cause). But see **attitude arrest.** From David M. Boatright, instructor, Texas Peace Officer Laws class, Austin TX Community College, 1993.

cooking freebase—"Trafficker's expression for process of eliminating the pesky hydrochloride from cocaine" (which makes it easier to smoke.) The crude way is "melting a mixture of cocaine and baking soda together over a flame. Any big spoon and any sustained flame would do. Then he scraped and scraped the solidified rock until all of it was reduced to fine, smokable powder." The more sophisticated way: "dissolving baking soda in water, bringing it to a boil, then adding a measure of cocaine. As the solution cooled, the insoluble cocaine base floated to the top in an oily film and coalesced in the center. When it solidified, he mortared or scraped it into a fine smokable powder." From Poppa, *Drug Lord.*

coop—a verb, meaning "to lie down on the job." "Back in those days when people cooped, rather than coop I would be on a rooftop looking for somebody selling junk or something."—Count, *Cop Talk.*

cop—originally a derogatory term for police, but more generally accepted, even within law enforcement, as its original meaning has faded with time. Long said to have been derived from "copper," a reference to the cheaper material used for badges of local police, as compared with the silver badges of the federal or state troopers, Paul Beale's *Partridge* traces it instead to the French and Latin, with the meaning "to take, steal, or make an arrest." (Fr. *caper* to seize). Police themselves classify cops as **bandits, standup guys,** and **corporate, by the bookers.**—Stroud, *Close Pursuit*, p. 49. Also known as **heat, fuzz, pigs** (most common during late 50s and 60s), **five-oh, flat-foot, Adam 12, the Man, human garbage collectors.**
As a verb, to "cop" can mean to "purchase or get drugs." It has been said to stand for "constable on patrol."

cop a plea—plead guilty, for favors or reduced sentence.

cop bar—bar where off duty police hang out. In Boston, usually an Irish bar—e. g. Foley's.

cop burn out—common depression suffered by veteran cops due to frustration of job, system, and constantly dealing with everyone's problems. Cycles of depression.

cop out—confess, inform, rat on.

cop shop—jocular term for a police station, but also any private investigation office which operates like a police station—"low on flash, high on results."—Parkhurst, *True Detectives* (p. 23).

cop 'stang—a police Ford Mustang. Often equipped with headers and bigger four-barrel carburetors, and possible a 351 engine instead of the stock 302.—from Poteet and Poteet, *Car & Motorcycle Slang* (Pigwhistle, 1992). See also **cruiser, Plain Jane, weight watcher.**

copycat crime—when a person commits a similar crime to a well-publicized earlier crime.

corner boy—street kid who hangs out buying, dealing drugs, stealing, hustling, or whatever.—Simon, *Homicide*, p. 449.

corpse cops—homicide detectives.—Joseph Wambaugh, *Fugitive Nights*, p. 51.

corpus delecti—"body of the crime." Evidence which proves that a crime occurred (all the elements of the crime."

cotton shot—drug-saturated cotton with water added to get leftover heroin.

cover and concealment—in tactical situations, police try to cover one another. Concealment is merely using an object to hide; cover refers to protection from gunfire as well.

cover thine ass—Police Department's First Commandment, according to Simon, *Homicide*, p. 321. **C. Y. A.**

crack—concentrated cocaine, **rocks,** also see **freebase.** More potent and addictive than regular cocaine itself.

crack house—apartment or house, often abandoned building, where users (**crack heads**) go to smoke crack.

crank—cheap **speed,** amphetamine.

cranked up—high on coke or speed.

crash squads—from the Los Angeles Police Department: these elite anti-gang units are criticized for becoming gang-like themselves, taunting gang members, celebrating gang members ' deaths with **kill parties**, **testilying** (lying in court to gain a conviction), even adopting the gangs' initiation ritual of testing newcomers to the unit with physical beatings. CRASH stands for Community Resources Against Street Hoodlums.

creeper—from Partridge, a **cat burglar**, i.e. a silent type who doesn't like to confront people. Still in use: in Joseph Wambaugh's *The Onion Field* (1973): "They couldn't be **boosters** or **creepers**, not flashing their bread like these two were doing."

a **crew**—a gang of young boys who have come together to engage in street crime as a unit.

crime dog—a gung-ho cop, making arrests, stopping crime, not just putting in time. "He solved the crime problem; he's a real crime dog." Sometimes used sarcastically about a lazy cop: "He hasn't made a collar in weeks!" "Who, O'Malley? Oh, he's a real crime dog!" A passionate crime fighter, a go-getter,also known as a **McGruff**, perhaps inspired by 1970s-80s television commercial featuring a cartoon dog, "McGruff the Crime Dog" whose expression was "take a bite out of crime."

crime magnet—an officer who comes a lot of crimes in progress, perhaps by hard work, but more than that—a seeming propensity to gravitate toward crimes. "Who, O'Shea? I don't want to work with him again. The guy's a fucking 'crime magnet.'"

crime scene unit—shortened to CSU, the term most often used to designate the "forensics" team. Early on the scene of any violent crime, NYPD.—Count, *Cop Talk.*

Crips—a major Los Angeles gang, rivals of the **Bloods**.

cross the line—begin to carry out police job unethically.

cross tops—amphetamine tablets with x on surface of pill (home made).

crows—in **SWAT team** operations, a term used to identify **perpetrators**, as distinguished from fellow officers (**eagles**), hostages (**canaries**), and persons who may go either way (**parrots**).

cruiser—marked police car.—from Poteet and Poteet, *Car & Motorcycle Slang* (iUniverse, 2000). See also **cop 'stang, Plain Jane, weight watcher.**

cruiser with berries flashing—street slang for cop car running with lights flashing. **Running hot** (from Ice Cube LP "Predator", song "A Good Day.")

crystal—methamphetamine.

cubehead—frequent user of LSD.

cuffed and stuffed—see **habeas grabus.** Jovial police description of an arrest (from Austin TX Police Department): "Two minutes after we got there, we had all three **perps** cuffed and stuffed!" Rhyming slang. "Cuffed" refers to "handcuffed;" "stuffed," to "thrown into the back of the police car."

cut—dilute, adulterate drugs by adding another inert substance, to increase profits.

cutter—medical examiner, coroner.

cutting corners—cop gets or is lazy and neglects certain necessities like concise and accurate paperwork and/or obtaining court order for arrest or search. Opposite of doing it **by the book** or **by the numbers.**

CYA—"Cover Your Ass, that's the number one rule in narcotics enforcement."—Goddard, *Undercover.* Age-old rule in law enforcement, actually. Mostly done by doing the job right, **by the book** or **by the numbers.** Not cutting corners. Documenting your actions or alleged actions with lots and lots of paperwork. See also **paper trail.**

cyclops—a car with one headlight out.

the **Dapper Don**—John Gotti, reputed head of New York Gambino family, Mafia, "untouched" by police operations for years because police couldn't make any charges "stick" to him, until right-hand man Sammy "The Bull" turned **rat** and handed over the Don.

Dan O'Leary, do a—to "work every minute of a tour," in the NYPD.—Anon., "Police Cant......oh yes they can!" *Spring 3100* (October 1958).

dart-out accidents—accidents which occur when a child runs, darts out, between parked cars and gets hit by a moving vehicle.—Fletcher, *Pure Cop*, p. 198.

D C D S—Deceased Confirmed Dead at Scene. Same as **DRT**—said of very obvious dead body, as opposed to **D O A.**

dead man—a new arrival on death row. "'Dead man comin' through.'"—Joseph Wambaugh's *The Onion Field.*

let's make a **deal**—police way to offer to **plea-bargain.** Usually initiates negotiation with one of several suspects to rat out on others.

decomp—dead body which has begun to decompose. See **rice.**

deep—"How deep are you in the city?"—"How many whores y'have?" "I'm only one deep."—Count, *Cop Talk.*

defence wounds—meaningful wounds on a corpse which tell the detective that the victim was being attacked and tried to defend him or herself, especially useful in cases where the murder has been staged to look like a suicide. See Simon, *Homicide,* p. 390. Also see *Criminal Investigation,* p. 292. Also called **defense cuts:** "deep slicing wounds usually found in the fingers, the palms, the wrists, and the forearms of a person who has been the victim of a knife attack."—Carsten Stroud, *Close Pursuit.*

de-knifed—took a knife away from.—from Ed Lennon, FHM.

desk jockey—police officer who doesn't work the street.

The Deuce—nickname for a consistently tough and sleazy area of NYC. 42 street between 6th and 9th avenues in Manhattan. See **Hell's Kitchen.**

deuce-less—a sentence of two years less a day, the maximum sentence for prisoners held in certain levels of provincial Canadian prisons.—Yates, *Line Screw.*

dex, dexies—dexedrine, an amphetamine.

dick—detective.

Dickless Tracy—a woman policeperson. Derived from the comic strip detective Dick Tracy, this term is not only sexist but seems to suggest that the original, Dick Tracy himself, had a macho which somehow escaped his readers; he seemed sexless, like Clark Kent ("Clark Bent"). In reaction against this view of women cops, see **Dirty Harriet Syndrome, Jane Wayne Syndrome.**—from Poteet and Poteet, *Car & Motorcycle Slang* (iUniverse, 2000).

dime bag—$10 bag of drugs (obsolete?)

dip—a pickpocket, a long-lasting slang term, as it is used in Dickens.

dirtbag, hairball, maggot, shithead, dogturd, slimebag, peckerwood (Texas), **skels, mutts, perps, scumbag**—various police terms of endearment for criminals.

Dirty Harriet Syndrome—derived from "Dirty Harry" from the movies. See **Jane Wayne Syndrome,** but also **Dickless Tracy, secretaries with guns.**

dis, diss—street slang for "disrespect," "insult."

distraction thieves—"teams of upscale pickpockets operating in airports, theme parks, fancy resorts, and big-time sports events.....They specialize in creating distractions by dropping cash or staging loud arguments, then grabbing purses, briefcases, and baggage."—Newhouse News Service citing a confidential police report, 1993.

got a **divorce**—used when a patrol cop gets a new street partner. The closeness of the relationship between partners is exemplified in the tradition that a partner is always supposed to be ready to lay down his life to protect the partner.

dixie cup—a person who is considered disposable.—Susanna Moore, *In the Cut.*

do—seduce, have sex with. Also to arrest through undercover operation: meet, befriend, deal with, then bust. In other words, to fuck over (still sexual). See **buy/bust.**

D. O. A.—Dead on Arrival (usually in hospital). See **D. R. T.**

Doctor Feelgood—doctor who writes prescriptions for drug addicts.

dog-meat—prisoner attempting to escape from a penal institution.—Yates, *Line Screw*.

dog watch—nickname for the "graveyard shift," the late-night to early morning work assignment, among San Antonio police, because "there's no one on the street at that time of night except policemen and stray dogs."—David "Mike" Logsdon. "Dog watch" from ship talk is the half-watch in early evening set up to regulate the rotation of crews, an exception to the regular four-hour on, off watches.

doing a pound—"serving a five year prison term"—Special Fraud Squad glossary of abbreviations and jargon, New York City.

dollies—dolophine (methadone), a synthetic narcotic.

domestic—a family problem/violence necessitating police response.

donorcycles—an item from motorcycle talk, but also by accident investigators in Texas and the Midwest: because motorcycles are dangerous to ride, many riders end up giving their organs for medical use. See also Poteet and Poteet, *Car and Motorcycle Slang* and *Car Talk*.

don't shit where you live—detective's advice to stupid criminal.

do time, to go down the river—to spend time in jail. Also, as a cop, to spend time on the street.

done—dead or immobilized, as in beaten senseless. "Go ahead, stick a fork in him, he's done." "I'm sick of working him; he's done." Or, "has no more information to yield to interrogator."

door shakers—regular cop's contemptuous tag for private security cops, suggesting that all they do is check locked offices. See also **Mickey Mouse ....., Rent-a-Pig, no-badge, sweetchuck.**

do- rag—street slang for a tight head scarf.

double tap—see **press-up.**

the **double whammy**—police slang for situation where a person suffers two really painful losses at the same time (loses job, wife left him), which causes him to flip out and creates **HBT** incident. See **stressor.**

downers—depressant drugs, barbiturates.

down for mine—"able to protect myself, as in 'I'll be fine; I be down for mine.'"—Susanna Moore, *In the Cut.*

Drag worm—in Austin, Texas, where the part of Guadalupe Street that runs along the campus of the University of Texas is known as "the drag," a "drag worm" was in police terminology a homeless person, a panhandler, along that strip.

Dr. Death—Dr. Kevorkian, activist practitioner of euthanasia, from Michigan. See also the verb "to **kevorkian,**" **medecide.**

drifting—method of safecracking; see the **Punch.**

drilling—use of high torque drill with diamond or carbide-tipped bits to break into safe. See also **blasting, burning, the rip.**

drive-by shooting—type of assault/execution/terrorizing attempt characteristic of U. S. urban gang wars. Also called simply a **drive-by.** See also **walk by.**

drop—swallow a drug.
> —getting gun out and pointed towards perp first, before he gets "the drop" on you.
> —place where kidnap ransom money is left or exchanged. "The drop." The action of making the exchanged.

drop a dime—"to provide information to the police about a specific crime, originally to make a call to the cops".—Stroud, *Close Pursuit,* p. 330.

drop gun—"nonofficial weapon carried by officer," presumably to drop at the scene of an incident in which police shot suspect, to establish guilt and cause of shooting.—Roth, *The Writer's Complete Crime Reference Book* (Cincinnati, OH: Writer's Digest Books, 1990). "A junk pistol usually confiscated from a criminal and carried by some police officers as a means of justifying a dubious shooting."—Stroud, *Close Pursuit*, p. 330. Also known as a **throwdown gun.**

dropsy syndrome—"In dropsy cases, officers justify a search by the oldest of means: they lie about the facts. 'As I was coming around the corner I saw the defendant drop the drugs on the sidewalk, so I arrested him.'"—Heilbroner, *Rough Justice.*

D. R. T.—Dead Right There. Black humor variant on **D. O. A.** "Yeah, we found him **D. R. T.**" See Austin *Chronicle*, Dec. 18, 1992, p. 18. Obviously dead, as in case where officer finds head of driver in back seat of car. As opposed to DOA (dead on arrival, at hospital).

drug burn—a case of dishonor among thieves, this refers to cheating someone by pretending to deliver drugs, collecting the cash, but not delivering or delivering a short or weak or impure product.

drug lord—a major drug supplier.

drug pipeline—drug smuggling route or source.

drug store—apartment used to manufacture street drugs like crack, heroin, etc. See **crack house.**

drum—prison word for "cell." Also known as a "house," but, according to Yates, in *Line Screw*, never called a "cell."

dry dive—jumping off a building top. See **jumper.**

dry firing—practicing aiming and firing a weapon without bullets in it.—Wambaugh, *Lines and Shadows,* p. 45.

DT—street abbreviation for "detective." Stroud, *Close Pursuit,* p. 101. "Man, I"m telling you, those two dudes are DTs."

duck—"abandoned stolen vehicle. Usually identifiable by a conspicuous lack of parts, like seats and engines, or by a forest of parking tickets. 'Let's impound that **duck**; It'll be worth an hour's overtime.'"—"L. A. Speak," *Los Angeles Times Magazine*, March 26, 1995.

duke—hand. This bit of pickpocket slang explains the otherwise cryptic but well-known "Put up your dukes!" as a legendary challenge to a fist-fight. See **shading the duke**.

duke man—"a stall who blocks view as pickpocket removes wallet." Hence **shading the duke**—Anon., "Police Cant......oh yes they can!" *Spring 3100* (October 1958).

dump job—an instance of someone's having had to dispose of a body. A murder case where person is killed in one place and then body is dumped in another place. Hard to solve because crime scene is unknown to detective (little or no physical evidence exists).

dunkers—detective slang for homicide cases that virtually solve themselves, are easy to solve. Cases accompanied by ample evidence and an obvious suspect (such as a domestic murder: man kills wife). The opposite is a **whodunit**. See also **red balls**.—from David Simon's *Homicide*.

duping operation—"duplicating operation": "process in which a vehicle (late model) is destroyed by accident, fire, etc. Owner collects insurance and vehicle sold to salvage yard where it is sold for parts. Paperwork-registration etc. purchased by stolen car ring and a vehicle matching the destroyed vehicle is stolen and paperwork switched."—Special Fraud Squad glossary of abbreviations and jargon, New York City.

D W H U A—Driving with Head Up Ass. Police joke variant on DWI (driving while intoxicated). See also **A L J**.

Eagle—criminal or cop who works alone.

eagles—SWAT team term for one of their own, in a description, say, on the radio, summing up a situation. "Three eagles have control; five **crows** identified; sixty **canaries** and possibly two **parrots**."

Ecstasy—synthetic psychotropic drug popular with **Rave** goers. Also known as MDA, MDMA, XTC, X, E, and many other names..

E D P—cop shorthand for "emotionally disturbed person," used of anyone upset, crazy, or pissed off.

eight ball—three and a half grams of cocaine, drug culture slang for an eighth of an ounce.

eighty-sixed—killed, also **punched his ticket, snuffed out**....—Stroud, *Close Pursuit*, p. 161.

Eliot Ness syndrome—famous gangbuster, anti-crime-boss FBI **crime dog** gave his name to this attitude and purposeful activity—from Petevich, *To Live & Die in L. A., Shakedown*. Often sarcastic, a remark about a cop with an exaggerated opinion of his ability to solve crime problem or bring down organized crime. The sarcasm may also come from the legend, still current among Chicago police, that he "never fired his gun except on the [firing] range!"

enforcement rationale—a reason why a policeman looks further into a situation, not necessarily a violation of the law or an action strictly chargeable. For example, **ALJ, black in a no-black zone** (or "poor in a no-poor zone, homeless in a no-homeless zone, etc.), **POPO, contempt of cop**.

E. T. A.—many jocular uses of this abbreviation, for "estimated time of arrival." E. g. : "What's the E T A on that hamburger, Joe? I gotta get back out there and keep the streets safe for our citizens."

ex-con—a person who has "done time" in prison.

Explorers Club—group of people who take LSD together. See **trip.**

eyefuck—to try to intimidate a witness with stares, bold aggressive looks, in the courtroom (or in the street). From Simon, *Homicide*, p. 281. Also known as **hairy eyeball, evil eye.**

eye in the sky—police helicopter.

fade, do the—because of sensing danger, to disappear from a crime scene unobtrusively.

fade heat—(v.) to ride trouble out, to keep your job; "a good supervisor backs up his men."

fag factory—prison, seen as a place which creates homosexuals.

fag hag—term for a woman who hangs around with gay men.

fall guy—a person who is set up to take the blame for a crime.

family albums—a set of photobooks which the NYPD homicide course squadroom keeps with the gristliest shots of victims, to show candidates, to see whether they can take it.

farebeat—NYC misdemeanor, riding the subway without paying.— David Heilbroner, *Rough Justice.*

fast change scam—a scheme to cheat a gullible person out of money. Person uses pretense of being a hurry, e. g. and distraction to confuse cashier into giving incorrect excessive change on purchase. Also known as a **quick change scam.** See also **con game, confidence game.**

Father Mulcahy syndrome—According to Philbin, "a police response to an emergency situation that is based more on the movies than on proper training." He quotes Connie Fletcher's *Pure Cop*, who claims that Jimmy Cagney/Barry Fitzgerald movies influenced inexperienced cops to reflexively make wrong moves, like "get a priest. get the mother. get the father. put them all on the phone. leave my gun outside. exchange myself for the kid. ....which gets people killed."

F. B. I.—officially Federal Bureau of Investigation, the acronym has spawned a number of city cop jokes about the **feds**: Forever Bothering Italians, and Famous But Incompetent.

fecal gravity—the chain of command defined. ("Shit rolls downhill").—Simon, *Homicide,* p. 45.

feds—short for "federal police officers," such as **FBI**, DEA, ATF, US Treasury. Also **G-Men** (government men).

feebie—from "FBI," a **fed,** a member of the Federal Bureau of Investigation.—Dean Thompson, DFW Airport **SWAT** sergeant.

The **felony ecology of the streets**—Marcus Laffey's memorable summary phrase for the synoptic description of drug dealing arrangements, personnel, etc.

fence—receiver of stolen goods who resells them.

fender lizards—San Antonio police slang term for women who hang around police, police groupies, because "they're always leaning on the fenders of the police car.

fiend—"to throw a choke hold on a victim."—Stroud, *Close Pursuit,* p. 331.

finger—to point out, or otherwise identify the person guilty of a crime, to the police. See also **snitch, squeal, rat, sing,** etc.

fink—old word for "rat," squeal," i. e. inform.

firefight—shootout. From military talk.

Fireman's Friend—see **firesetter, torch.**

firesetter—arsonist, "fireman's friend" (ironic). "Arson investigators note that firesetters are often at the scene of the fire they set, helping the fireman, the police, giving information, rolling up hoses, offering all kinds of help: the Fireman's Friend."—Fletcher, *Pure Cop*, p. 49.

fish—a new prisoner, **a greenie, a virgin.** "I hear there's a new virgin in C-Block."

fish and shrimp—for pimp.

five-oh—gang street talk to call out as a warning that the cops are coming. From "Hawaii 5-0".—from Petevich, *To Live & Die in L. A., Shakedown.*

five by five—"You are coming in loud and clear."—Stroud, *Close Pursuit,* p. 331.

five-finger discount—what you get when you shoplift and get away with it.

fixer—"any location where a P. O. remains in permanent attendance, usually in a booth."—Carsten Stroud, *Close Pursuit.*

flake—to plant evidence to get a conviction. "Isn't it a fact that you put that gun in the ceiling and planted it on my client....cause you wanted to flake my client?"—Count, *Cop Talk.* "To plant evidence, usually a gun."—Susanna Moore, *In the Cut.*

flaming shit bomb—paper bag of excrement, set on fire and dropped on cops, makes the officers earn their bonuses and does not help their attitude. See also **Nair bomb.**

flash bang—a concussion grenade, known to the British as a **flash crash.**

flasher—a person who exposes himself in public.

flash the tin—officer shows badge to gain access to restricted area or otherwise identify himself. In Chicago, **put the button on him** means the same thing.

flash money, flash wad—cash used by undercover cops to show ("flash") to bad guys and suggest that they are, not cops, but big time crooks.

flex cuffs, flex-cuf ties, riot cuffs—durable, flexible plastic ties used to handcuff prisoners when regular cuffs are not readily available or plentiful, as in a riot.

flip—turn informant.

flip, flip out—become violent, psychotic, upset.

floaters—dead bodies in the water.—from Bill Kelly's *Street Dance*.

fly—"to be temporarily assigned to another command."—Special Fraud Squad glossary of abbreviations and jargon, New York City.

footbath—"mobster technique of forcing victim to put feet into bucket of cement before being tossed overboard."—De Sola, p. 58. See **cement overshoes.**

for your safety and ours—police phrase to explain need to handcuff arrested suspects.

frame—1. to make an innocent person appear guilty of a crime. See **plant.**
2. "to place a victim in a position to have his pockets picked." (NYPD)—Anon., "Police Cant......oh yes they can!" *Spring 3100* (October 1958).

free ride—an arrested person getting off without doing any time, i.e. by dismissal, probation, charges dropped, etc.—Heilbroner, *Rough Justice*.

freon freak—someone who inhales freon gas. Also **frost freak.** Nash.

fresh—well-dressed, cool, up-to-date, an obvious likely **vic.**—Stroud, *Close Pursuit,* p. 98.

friendly fire—refers to being shot accidentally by a fellow police officer. Also used in military talk.

frisk—to search a suspect.

frog and feather—code for wallet or pocketbook. Rhymes with leather.

front—sell with promise of payment to come. To provide for sale, trusting the purchaser to make good on the debt. Also in organized crime, legitimate, legal business establishment which is used to conceal illegal activities, "launder" money, etc.

fruit hustler—male prostitute for gay men.—Curtis Gray, Chicago.

fruit machine—a device used by the government of Canada during the 1960s to root out homosexuals in the civil service. "An individual peered into the narrow opening of a large box in which sometimes lewd pictures from magazines were shown. A camera recorded pupil size as each new image was flashed."—Montréal *Gazette*, April 24, 1992.

fuck—said to be originally from the way San Francisco cops charged prostitutes in the 19th Century : For Unlawful Carnal Knowledge.

fudge packer bar—see **buttslam bar.**

full float—recovered stolen auto with no wheels.—Curtis Gray, Chicago.

full moon theory of inner-city mortality—like the **summer heat-wave theory,** an explanation of increased violence at certain times. Among police officers, the worst combination is said to be the coming together of full moon, payday, and Saturday night.

doing the **funky chicken**—cop slang for someone in struggle just before passing out from the carotid artery hold immobilization technique, or someone in death throes.—From Simon, *Homicide*, p. 317. The phrase signals to the officer, "stop," as the immobilization is working and there is danger of injury to the person being brought under control. See **choke hold.**

funny money—counterfeit money.

fuzz—derogatory, very old term for police. Speculations on the origin of this term are diverse. Morris' *Dictionary of Contemporary Usage* claims it may be traced to the 1920s when U. S. federal narcotics agents were called "feds," and that "the theory is that the whispered 'Feds!' as warning of an impending raid could easily be corrupted into 'fuzz.'" But Stewart Beach found it used as a term for a British policeman in an Edgar Wallace novel of 1915. And Eric Partridge only cites a 1950s Canadian jazz source. It may be originally from the time when U.S. FBI and revenue agents wore full beards; so to insult a young, local cop, you'd call him "fuzz," as in "peach fuzz," implying that he was too young to grow a beard. Also has been explained as coming from the fuzz that came off the wool suit that police wore. Derivative: "fuzz that wuz," a former cop (derogatory). See also the **heat, pigs, cops, five-oh, Adam 12, the Man, human garbage collectors.**

gag—to shut someone up, to keep them from talking.

gang bangers—gang members on a cruise. Also, active gang members.—from police taping/special on juvenile delinquents, Austin Cablevision '93.

gangster lean—"the cool way to sit in the driver's seat of a car, leaning to the window side."—Susanna Moore, *In the Cut.*

gash—"a white woman who has been raped."—Carsten Stroud, *Close Pursuit.*

gat—very old word for a handgun.

gate—release from prison.

get busy—street slang for "to rob someone."

get up—to spray gang symbol all over the 'hood, to mark allegiance on the turf. Black talk in criminal and cop talk.

ghetto bird—LA street name for police helicopter constantly seen flying over problem areas with spotlights and PA system.

ghost—a narcotics officer, for the "plain clothes" which make him or her invisible.—Count, *Cop Talk.*

glory hole—hole in public bathroom stall, usually in gay bar or hangout, where patron can receive anonymous blowjob.

go—street for fight. "Wanna go?"

go ahead, make my day—dare or taunt much used, implying that if the suspect would make any threatening move or move to escape, the cop would enjoy immensely the use of force justified by such action. From Clint Eastwood's seasoned-cop character Dirty Harry.

godmother—"An Ottawa crime family referred to Montreal Mountie as being their 'godmother,' a term used for a corrupt cop.—Montréal *Gazette* (January 17, 1993).

go downtown—be arrested or brought to police station for questioning. "Look, pal, you're going downtown if we don't get some straight answers out of you right now."

gold shield—"detective's shield."—Special Fraud Squad glossary of abbreviations and jargon, New York City. Often abbreviated to **gold**, as distinguished from **tin**.

good guy-bad guy technique—see **Mutt and Jeff routine**. Common police detective technique in which one cop seems to sympathize and befriend suspect, while other cop terrorizes him. "You better tell him what you know soon, because I don't know how much longer I can hold him back. I've never seen him this angry before....Last time he nearly killed the suspect."

goulash house—cop name for after-hours joint featuring all the vices: booze, gambling, hookers, and drugs.—McCarthy, *Vice Cop.*

go up on a bomb—bomb squad expression for act of approaching a bomb to dismantle it. Also **on top of a bomb.**—Fletcher, *Pure Cop*, p. 1.

goyakod—Get Off Your Ass and Knock On Doors, "questioning of potential witnesses of a crime...In NYC, one highly experienced homicide sergeant was heard to say that nothing beats 'goyakod' in an investigation."—Philbin, p. 103.

grass eaters—one of two categories of New York City policemen "on the take," i. e. actively taking bribes. This group "passively accepted whatever cash fell their way."—McCarthy, *Vice Cop,* p. 43. To be distinguished from **meat eaters.**

graveyard shift—the midnight to 8 a.m. shift, characterized from the police point of view as a shift on which much less crime happens than between 4 p.m. and midnight. See **vampires.**

grease-trap theory—"the view, put forth by some resident law officers, that Florida's high incidence of violent crime is tied to the migration into the state of thousands of people a week, some of whom are or become criminals. 'Detectives across the state say....when the weather up north starts turning cold, the scum start moving south. [They] believe that Florida's climate and location draw a disproportionate share of people on the run.'"—Anne Soukhanov, "Word Watch," *Atlantic Monthly* (February 1994).

green, greenshoe—a rookie cop. Cadets wear olive-black shoes. A naïve cop in training. "Green" is a common slang term for fresh, new, not seasoned, even applying to newly made aircraft (see Poteet and Stone, *Plane Talk*.)

greenies—amphetamine tablets (oval shaped).

green onion—parking meter officers in Montréal, from the color of their uniforms. **Meter maids.**

grounder, hanger—"an easy case. E. g. 'I just caught a grounder.'"— Special Fraud Squad glossary of abbreviations and jargon, New York City.

The opposite of an easy case to solve (grounder) is a **mystery**, according to Carsten Stroud, *Close Pursuit*, p. 269. Compare the Baltimore distinction between **dunkers** and **whodunits**. The sports background of these two sets of slang terms (baseball and basketball) is obvious; a "grounder" is a ball hit into the infield for an easy out; a "hanger" was a hanging curve ball that because it didn't curve away properly, was easy to hit hard and far.

gumball—a police car with a single overhead light.

gump—male transvestitute prostitute, which make up about 60% of the street whore population, according to vice cops.—Fletcher, *Pure Cop,* p. 87.

gumshoe—a detective. Also **dick, snooper, snoop.**

gun run—NYPD radio term for an arrest involving firearms.—Stroud, *Close Pursuit*, p. 234.

gutter junkie—drug addict who relies on others to support habit. See **coke whore.**

gymnasium punk—a new arrival in prison who is used in homosexual multiple intercourse, not necessarily consensual: "The other guys bend him over a workout bar and **brown** him."—Joseph Wambaugh's *The Onion Field.*

gypsy bankroll—the wad of money, real bills on top only, for use in a **con game** or **buy-bust.**

habeas grabus—jocular variant on "habeas corpus," meaning "to arrest." "Habeas corpus" is of course the name of the writ a lawyer may get to force the police to release a suspect after a certain length of detention without charges being filed. It is Latin for "we have the body." "We put the old habeas grabus on him!"—Austin TX Police Academy. Also reported from Honolulu Police Department. **Cuffed and stuffed.**

hacker—see **computer hack.**

hair bag—"veteran police officer; younger officer who attempts to create the impression that he is a veteran." (From "bag" as used to mean "police uniform").—Special Fraud Squad glossary of abbreviations and jargon, New York City.

hairy eyeball—see **eyefuck.**

handcuffs as bracelets—officer takes out handcuffs and tells unruly subject, "Unless you want to add these to your wardrobe, you better get the hell outta here." From Tim Sullivan, Faneuil Hall Marketplace security force, Boston.

handkerchief switch—"a scheme in which the victim is left with empty handkerchief after his money has been taken by a con man; also **confidence game, stuff, Jamaican switch, West Indian switch.**"—Special Fraud Squad glossary of abbreviations and jargon, New York City.

hands—"He's got good hands" means "he can fight."

hanging paper—passing counterfeit money. Petievich, *The Quality*

hanger binger—a pickpocket who specializes in stealing from shoulder-strap bags.—Edward Kirkman, "Wary of Perps & Shooflies, Cops Talk in Code," New York *Daily News* (November 12, 1974).

hard case—tough guy, or said of person who thinks he's tough. Stubborn, hard nut to crack, won't confess or talk. Also, a **hard guy.**

hard guy—Boston street expression for a tough person, or a person who thinks he's tough. Pronounced "hadd guy."

hard-on—to have a "hard-on" is to be obsessed with and or to dislike someone.

hardware—guns.

hash marks—scars on inside of wrists, a sign of one's having attempted suicide. **Hesitation marks.**

hawk—old for cheat or confidence man. Nash.

hawking a queer—beating up a gay person.—Elmore Leonard, *City Primeval,* p. 19.

H B T—"Hostage/Barricaded/Terrorist" unit, including hostage negotiators and containment officers (aka **SWAT team**).

head—dope user.

headhunter—internal affairs officer, a **suit** who tries to get other officers in trouble.

head shapes—A veteran white detective's scientific analysis of homeboy head shapes: "....now your bullet head, he's a stone killer, he's dangerous. But your peanut heads, they're just dope dealers and sneak thieves. Now your swayback he's generally a ......"—Simon, *Homicide,* p. 506.

head shop—store which sells drug paraphernalia.

heater—gun, also **gat.**

Heavenly Blues—a type of morning glory seeds, a drug source.

hello phones—lines used by mob informers to reach their contacts in the FBI. The name comes from the cops' saying "hello" first, rather than their name.

Hell's Kitchen—nickname for mid-west side of NYC.

helping a case—a cop lying to ensure a conviction when he knows the perp is guilty but might not otherwise be able to convince the jury.—from NYPD Blue, 04/12/94.

henchmen—hired muscle, strongmen, killers.

the **"he needed killing" defense**—an actual "yes, but" defense to homicide in the State of Texas. Supposedly, if defense can prove that the murder victim was so bad that he actually "had it coming to him," this should lessen the murderer's culpability or degree of guilt.

hep—in street talk, an old term meaning "aware," which may have been "criminal slang from the name of a top-notch detective who worked in Cincinnati (1914). On the other hand, *American Speech* noted in 1941, 'Tis said that back in the 1890s, Joe Hep ran a saloon in Chicago....Although he never quite understood what was going on, he thought he did....Hence his name entered the argot as an ironic appellation.'"—"Social Studies," Toronto *Globe and Mail* (March 1994).

he/she—a noun, police slang term for a transvestite, a crossdresser.

Also known as a **shim.**

hesitation marks—often found on suicide victims, as a series of lesser wounds inflicted by the victim which are in the same general region of the fatal wound, wrists, forearms, throat..... See also **hash marks.**

heroin—junk, scag, horse, white horse, smack.

hide—(n.) girl/boyfriend. Also **chips.**

high priced spreads—expensive hookers.

highrisers—on New York State Highway Patrol cars, "a light that comes up straight so you can see them from a distance."—Count, *Cop Talk.*

hinky—"There was something very weird about him, something way off. He was a little 'hinky,' [Johanna] Gerbrands said." "'Hinky' is a word police use to describe a 'weird' person."—Austin TX police officer describing someone who confessed to 14 rapes. This perception is referred to, sometimes, as "spider-sense," from Spiderman (Marvel Comic hero) who had a kind of extra-sensory perception of evil. "Man, my spider-sense was ringing on that one.

hit, strike, or **match**—said when comparison of records in computer reveals positive or identical (e. g. fingerprints). **Bingo.**

hit the wire—tried to escape.—Los Angeles prison guard talk.

holding—having drugs in one's possession.

holed up—hiding out. Though this is a fairly common metaphor, its use by cops and street criminals suggests the imagery of rats, prey, etc., human vermin....

homeboy—"He's one of my homeboys, I came up with him." Black slang for friend or fellow gang member. A person from the neighborhood.

homicide—the killing of a human being by another human being. See also **murder.**

homicide lexicon rule 24/24—The most important hours in a murder investigation are the last twenty-four hours in the victim's life and the first twenty-four hours after the body is discovered. "The secret of the killing lies in this time zone. Go back beyond that and the forces that led to his death are too diffuse, and after the first 24 hours the witnesses are starting to forget things; the tissues are drying out; the weapons are being destroyed. Clothes are being burned and stories are being agreed upon."—Stroud, *Close Pursuit*, p. 18, 19.

hook—an "influential friend who makes the phone call to the C. O.(Commanding Officer)" to get someone into a high-intensity training program and squad like "forensics,' NYPD.—Count, *Cop Talk*.

hooked—addicted to drugs. Also police expression for when a target of an undercover operation is sucked in, believes operative is a buyer and his greed causes him to risk dealing with someone he obviously doesn't know very well (or he'd know he was a cop).

hopped up—under the influence of narcotics like cocaine or PCP.

horse—heroin. "All horsed out" means "high on heroin."

horse race—a couple observed having sex in a relatively public place. "Hey, guys, there's a horse race behind building 3!"—overheard on the two-way radio at Faneuil Hall Marketplace Security.

hot—stolen. A "hot" car is a stolen car.

hot and cold—refers to dangerous practice of taking a depressant and a stimulant successively. Eg, heroin and cocaine. See **speedball**.

hot dogs—prison-issue shoes worn on release.—Joseph Wambaugh, *The Onion Field*.

hot load, hot shot—a dose of pure heroin, which is lethal. Or a lethal drug dose of heroin mixed with strychnine or cyanide.

hot rocks—stolen gems/jewels.

hot rod—a modified gun, to make it easier to shoot (wider trigger), or with safety features removed. Also a verb. Usually it is police who do this.

hot roller—stolen car being driven by thieves.—Wambaugh, *The New Centurions.*

hot seat—witness stand. Also electric chair.

hot sheet—list of vehicles recently stolen in area, given or read to patrol officers before shift.

hot shot—1. "high-priority or emergency radio calls."—"L. A. Speak," *Los Angeles Times Magazine*, March 26, 1995.
2. "an unexpectedly potent and therefore lethal hit of heroin." **Toxic smack.**—Stroud, *Close Pursuit,* p. 332.

hot wire—steal a car without the keys, usually done at the steering column.

Houdini, doin' the—"cutting up a body and discarding the pieces so they can't be identified," according to Philbin, p. 71. Refers to Harry Houdini, famous escape and illusion art around the turn of the century, before and after 1900.

housedogs—prison guard's term for prisoners for inmates who will "attach themselves to whichever power group they think will prevail."— Yates, *Line Screw.*

hubcaps—"detectives who investigate auto theft. 'I've been on **hubcaps** so long I think every car in L.A. has been stolen twice.'"—"L. A. Speak," *Los Angeles Times Magazine*, March 26, 1995.

huckaleros, hucks—"Shortly after El Dorado [a drug-fighting police task force] was founded, a Hispanic member of the task force began referring to the Colombians as 'huckaleros,' a term used for Mexicans in a John Wayne movie, and it stuck. To the members of the task force, Colombians are 'hucks.' 'Huck is redballed at Eight Three and Rosey' translates as 'the Colombian suspect is stopped at a red light on the corner of Eighty-third Street and Roosevelt Avenue."—Fredric Dannen, "Colombian Gold: Annals of Justice," *New Yorker*, Aug. 15, 1994.

huevos—see **balls to spare.**

to be **hung like a horse**—to have influential connections in the police department, also, to be hung like a horse!—Susanna Moore, *In the Cut.*

husband and wife—used in place of knife. See **boat and oar.** Nash.

hustle—activities involved in obtaining money to buy heroin. E. g. prostitution, dealing.

hustler—prostitute.

hype—narcotics addict.

ice—(as a verb), kill. A dead suspect is **iced, on a slab.**

ice—concentrated "speed" (methedrine, amphetamine). "What 'crack' is to coke, ice is to methedrine." Also "jewelry."

identity parade—according to Calvin Trillin in the New Yorker, the "courteous" British cop phrase for what in the U. S. is known as a **lineup.**

inching—to "inch" someone is to exact "a form of retributory punishment used by Jamaican drug dealers that involved the systematic hacking of arms and legs, inch by inch."—*Rough Justice.*

inflash—street talk, for "to inform," as in "he inflash me with the bitch's scenario."—Susanna Moore, *In the Cut.*

inner perimeter—in describing parts of a **kill zone** in an incident involving encounters with armed and dangerous individuals, the "inner perimeter" is the zone delimited by the inner ring of police keeping the bad guy in; the "outer perimeter" is the outer ring of police keeping uninvolved citizens out.—Fletcher, *Pure Cop*, p. 224.

in service/out of service—an officer is in service when he is in his patrol car ready to answer a call for assistance on radio. He is out of service while handling a call or problem. "Baker 202 out on traffic" means the officer, stopping a vehicle, is notifying dispatcher that he is handling a moving violation and cannot handle any calls.

in the bag—"wearing regulation uniform of the day; assignment to uniformed force."—Special Fraud Squad glossary of abbreviations and jargon, New York City.

jack and jill—cash register. Rhymes with till.

jailhouse lawyer—a prison inmate who knows criminal law and helps with other inmates' legal work.

Jakes—"uniformed police officers."—Roth, *The Writer's Complete Crime Reference Book.*

jammie—"a gun, perhaps of inferior make, one that jams?"—Susanna Moore, *In the Cut.*

Jane Wayne Syndrome—the tendency of new women police recruits to overact, be extra tough, to show that they can compete with the men. Also known as **Dirty Harriet Syndrome.** For the same syndrome among men, see **John Wayne syndrome, badge-heavy.**

Jaws of Life—rescue tool; hydraulically actuated spreading tool that goes into metal to enlarge openings, such as to open jammed car doors, so that a trapped driver or passenger can get free of wreckage.—from Poteet and Poteet, *Car & Motorcycle Slang* (Ayers Cliff, Quebec: iUniverse, 2000).

jay—marijuana cigarette.

Jewish bankroll—wad of money made to seem larger by counterfeit money in the middle. See **gypsy bankroll.**

Jewish lightning—"arson," according to Philbin. "Most likely arose during the '30s or 40's when bias against Jews was strong and vocal, particularly related to money. P. 130. See also **Mexican lightning.**

the job—how police refer to being a cop. "I get paid for this, too?"

jocker—older homosexual initiator of young juvenile offender, in prison.—Joseph Wambaugh, *The Onion Field.*

john—man who hires prostitute.

John Doe, Jane Doe—names used for reporting purposes where subject's name is unknown. See also **members of the deer family.**

the John Squad—undercover vice squad.—Joseph Wambaugh, *Fugitive Nights,* p. 56.

joint—a marijuana cigarette.

the Joint—prison.

jolly beans—pep pills, uppers, amphetamines, speed.

jostle operation—a two-perp operation where one bumps into victim to distract her, while other one pickpockets.—Stroud, *Close Pursuit,* p. 208.

juice—money, especially cash, to pay off people.—from Petevich, *To Live & Die in L. A., Shakedown.* Also, in the movie "Juice," by Ernest R. Dickerson, a term for power and respect among street gangs.

juicing—using anabolic steroids.

jump bail—fail to show up for court after bailbondsman has posted bail for defendant.

jumper—police slang for a person who threatens to jump off a building, bridge, etc. to commit suicide.

jumping in—gang initiation in which members physically beat new recruits to establish that they are tough enough to join the gang. See **the line.**

junk—heroin.

junkies—heroin addicts.

kevorkian (v.)—to perform **medecide,** a medically assisted suicide. Named for the well-known activist physician Dr. Kevorkian of Michigan, an advocate and practitioner of enthanasia. **Dr. Death.**

kick—quit drugs.

kicking ass and taking names—successful police arrest or operation or brawl. "I heard you guys were kicking ass and taking names over in Charlie sector last night." This phrase appears in Wambaugh's *Lines and Shadows,* p. 33. "'From a prosecutorial standpont, we're slaughtering 'em,' Gleeson said. 'We're kickin' ass and takin' names.'"—Fredric Dannen, "Annals of Law: Defending the Mafia," *New Yorker* (February 21, 1994).

kicking cold—ceasing drug use without medical support.

killer weed—marijuana spiked with PCP.

kill parties—"The L. A. police taunt [the LA gangs] in Rampart by driving around with handcuffs swinging from their rear-view mirror, or occasionally holding 'kill parties' to celebrate gang killings."—Peter Goodspeed. "In L.A., a land outside the law," *National Post* (Thursday, November 25, 1999).

kill zone—area in which offender can get a clear shot at you. See **inner perimeter, outer perimeter.**

kiting a check—writing a check that is no good and persuading someone to cash it, thus flying it for money before it comes to rest and is revealed as fraudulent.

kneecapping—underworld form of punishment in which the victim's knee is shot or hit with a baseball bat or other weapon.

knob-knocking—see the **Punch.**

knocked—street slang for "getting arrested."—Stroud, *Close Pursuit, 333.*

knuckledraggers—big burly guys, according to David Sedgwick, Westmount, Québec Auxiliary Police force; "down in Texas, they've got mostly 'knuckledraggers' for cops, eh?"

koolaid—LSD, Acid.

Lajaras—"Hispanic slang for a policeman; after O'Hara."—Carsten Stroud, *Close Pursuit,* p. 333. Northeastern U.S.

landline—telephone, as distinguished from radio.

la plaza—"Quien esta manieando la plaza?" "Usually refers to a police authority and his jurisdiction. To the Mexican drug underworld, however, it has a separate and very precise meaning: 'Who has the concession to run the narcotics racket?' To have the "plaza" meant that he was paying an authority or authorities with sufficient power to ensure that he would not be bothered by state or federal police or by the military.—Terrence E. Poppa, *Drug Lord,* p. 40.

LCC—last cover and concealment, a point marked by SWAT team members as part of the routine of **breeching** or "making an entry."

lean on him—threaten him, intimidate him, pressure an individual to confess or give information about a crime.

lemonade—poor grade heroin.

lie box—polygraph instrument ("lie detector.")

lies—"Rule Number One in a death investigation: everyone lies."—D. Simon, H*omicide.*

lift—to steal, or **boost.**

Lindbergh Law—imposed the death penalty for a kidnapping. "Means death....it's them or us."—Joseph Wambaugh, *The Onion Field.*

line, the—street gang rite of initiation, in which would-be new gang member has to proceed through a narrow corridor made up of his fellow gang members, who punch, kick, and strike him with weapons until he emerges at the end and is then a full-fledged member.

line screw—prison guard.

lineup—investigative procedure whereby a witness to a crime observes a group of persons, including some suspects and some who are not, through one-way glass or mirror, to see if identification may be made positively.

See also **identity parade.**

liquid courage—alcohol induced bravery. Like **beer muscles.**

liquid sky—heroin. See **blue sky.**

live Mish—"a large amount of $1 bills with a large denomination bill on the top and bottom of the stack; also **Michigan roll.**"—Special Fraud Squad glossary of abbreviations and jargon, New York City. See also **gypsy bankroll, Jewish bankroll.**

Lojack—antitheft device for cars which basically plants a homing bug on the vehicle which can be activated when car is stolen so that police can track the car - very effective. See **Rat Trap.**

lollipop gangsters—Feds name for new breed of Mafia, sons of tough Mafia bosses who grew up in affluence, unlike their old-school fathers who fought their way to the top of La Cosa Nostra. These kids inherited their fathers' organizations but did not have the same ruthlessness and have arguably weakened the organization.—Boston *Globe*, Dec. 4,5, 1991.

lone wolf—detective cop who works best alone.

'Ludes—"Quaaludes, a soporific, also known as the Breakfast of Losers."—Carsten Stroud, *Close Pursuit*.

MAB—"missing at birth; used to explain deformity on police fingerprint forms."—Special Fraud Squad glossary of abbreviations and jargon, New York City. See also **AMP**.

mack man—from the 1920s, NYC, a pimp.—Count, *Cop Talk*.

made—in police slang, "recognized." "I'm going to have to pull out (of this under cover operation). I think one of them 'made' me (as a cop) last night—I arrested him two years ago." But in underworld slang, especially among the Cosa Nostra (Mafia), means **connected**, accepted

as a member of the Mafia, is a full-blown Mafia family member. Also known as a **wiseguy.**
In the NYPD, means "promoted." "If you made page 4 of the Daily News, you had your shield. To **get made** you gotta have that **hook**—someone to put in a word for you."—E. W. Count, *Cop Talk.*

maggot farm—decomposed body.

mainline—to inject drugs into a vein.

make—to identify a police officer who is working undercover. Also for a police action of recognizing offender and getting warrant for arrrest.

mama bear—"female officer" (truckers' slang)—Roth, *The Writer's Complete Crime Reference Book.* See also **Dickless Tracy, badge on a beaver, Charlie's Angel, Jane Wayne syndrome, Dirty Harriet syndrome.**

man, the—street name for police.

man down—radio code phrase to identify a call involving person injured (on the ground), shot, drunk.....
    2. in Los Angeles prison guard talk: "epileptic seizure."

Manhattan make it, Harlem take it—an explanation of mugging in New York City.—Stroud, *Close Pursuit,* p. 98.

manipulation—safe break using senses to hear or feel the tumblers of combination lock falling into position. Rare, despite all its occurrences in crime movies.

mark—person whom undercover operation or con game is targeting.

marked up—showing visible signs of injury, suggesting cops or somebody beat person.

masher, leg breaker, goon—hired muscle, a guy paid for his brawn, not his brains.

mass murderer—person who kills multiple victims in one violent blood-bath slaying. Usually is killed or kills self before apprehended.

Masterbadge—like a Mastercard, a reference to the idea that you may flash the badge and "get anything for free." "I don't need any money for dinner; I'll just use my Masterbadge."

Mayberry Police Department—an ill-equipped, small-town, poorly trained police department. From the Andy Griffith Show.

meat eaters—one of two categories of New York City policemen "on the take," i. e. taking bribes. These are cops who "actively put the bite on any hand they saw."—McCarthy, *Vice Cop*, p. 43. To be distinguished from **grass eaters**.

meat-gazer—men's room peeping Tom. From Joe Lomuscio, former Faneuil Hall Marketplace security staff, Boston.

meat wagon—vehicle for picking up dead bodies to bring them to the morgue.

mechanic—1. skilled card cheater.—Polsky, *Hustlers, Beats and Others,* p. 101.
—contract killer. See also **hitman**.

Mechanic, The—purported nickname of NYC cop known to specialize in beating up suspects, giving **tune ups.**—from CNN newscast 10/06/93.

medecide—illegal medical assisted suicide. See also **Kevorkian, Dr. Death.**

Mellow Drug of America—slang for MDA, ECSTASY.

member of the deer family—cop slang for a victim where name is unknown. "Just another member of the deer family," i. e. John or Jane Doe.
—Simon, *Homicide*, p. 436.

mesc—mescaline, the alkaloid in peyote.

meth—methamphetamine, speed.

meth monster—person who experiences a violent reaction to **meth**.

Mexican lightning—like **Jewish lightning** in New York in the '30s and, 40s—"arson," especially in the southwest or West, where prejudice pointed to Mexicans in such fraud schemes.

Mickey Mouse security guard—a derogatory name for security guard or private police. See also **Rent-a-Pig, no-badge, door shakers, sweetchuck.**

middleman—person who introduces or runs go-between for buyer and seller in a drug deal or other criminal transaction.

miranda—widely used code word for the legal requirement that police inform a suspect being arrested of his or her rights. Named for the celebrated Supreme Court decision establishing this duty, *Miranda vs. Arizona* in 1966, with Earl Warren as Chief Justice.

mirandizing—informing a suspect of rights. "Mirandizing, as it came to be called, began with the immortal line, 'You have the right to remain silent.'"—Breo and Martin, *The Crime of the Century,* p. 131.

misdemeanor murder—a cynical way of labeling the murder of someone not very important, the opposite of a **red ball**. "Just another druggie whore, a misdemeanor murder." Homicide detective's way of revealing that some murder cases aren't as important as others, because of race, social status of victim, or lack of media attention.—From Austin TX *American-Statesman*, "Report Shakes Up Homicide Division," April 3, 1993. A similar tag is **N.H.I.** In fact, in Texas, criminally negligent homicide, as in, for example, causing death by reckless driving, was until September 1, 1994, a Class A misdemeanor. From David M. Boatright, instructor, Texas Peace Officer Laws class, Austin TX Community College, 1993.

moan and wail—for prison. Rhymes with jail.

M. O.—"modus operandi." Particular criminal's method of operation, certain aspects of a crime which mark it as a certain criminal's doings.

mol, moll—a female criminal or gangster's girlfriend. The source of the first name of Moll Flanders, heroine of Daniel Defoe's early 18th century ur-novel about a woman who has to turn to crime to survive (as well as marry five times). Still in use, according to the Kehilla Reports on Jewish life in New York's Lower East Side in the early use of the 20th century.

moll buzzer—a **dip** who steals from women.—Edward Kirkman, "Wary of Perps & Shooflies, Cops Talk in Code," New York *Daily News* (November 12, 1974).

molotov cocktail—homemade firebomb made by filling a bottle with flammable liquid and plugging it with a rag, which is lit and then the bottle thrown.

money laundering—attempt to conceal large amounts of cash profits from illegal enterprise by funneling them into a legitimate business.

mooner—"a person who goes bananas at the advent of a full moon."— Edward Kirkman, "Wary of Perps & Shooflies, Cops Talk in Code," New York *Daily News* (November 12, 1974).

mopery—minor offenses. "Gotti [crime boss] apparently sanctioned guilty pleas [among his employees] for what he called 'malicious mopery,' minor offenses that had nothing to do with the existence of La Cosa Nostra and did not affect other members of the family."—Fredric Dannen, "Annals of Law: Defending the Mafia," *New Yorker* (February 21, 1994). "'It's a malicious mopery, drunken-driving case, you'll get sixty days, you wanna take a plea? Take a plea.'"—John Gotti. Eric Partridge, *Underworld Slang*, defines "to mope" as "to dawdle, walk away."

mopes—(n.) cop's and prosecutor's contemptuous term for criminals. "He talks like an Irish cop: people he prosecutes are 'mopes' and 'pieces of shit.'"—Dannen. See also **mopery.**

move drugs—traffic, sell. "He's been moving about 100 pounds a month."

Mr. Stranger Danger—"a stranger who commits random sex crimes, [especially] a stranger who abducts and murders a child," according to Philbin, p. 154.

muff deal—a phrase used in San Antonio when a police officer suspects that the story offered to explain the incident is not the full story, that in fact the individuals involved in the problem (a break-in, an alleged rape, etc.) are known to each other, and that specifically there is a love or sexual relationship between them. The word "muff" also occurs in local slang in "to have the muffs," for "to be blindly in love," or "to have the screaming muffs for somebody," to be intensely in love or lust. "Muff" may be explicated clearly by remembering that "muff diver" is a women with a sexual preference for other women.

mugshot—standard police photos of arrested person, front and profile shots.

mule—a carrier, a lower-down employee or member of a drug importing gang, paid to transport drugs across borders. Terrence E. Poppa, *Drug Lord*, p. 9.

murder—the killing of a human being by another, with malice aforethought.

Murphy Game—"confidence game in which money is taken from victim on basis of a false promise that he will enjoy the services of a prostitute; perpetrated by 'Murphy men'".—Special Fraud Squad glossary of abbreviations and jargon, New York City.

mushroom—an innocent bystander killed during a shootout between police and suspects, so called because they spring up out of nowhere, are in the news one morning, then they disappear from sight.

Mutt and Jeff routine—also known as **the good guy-bad guy technique**, this procedure or strategy in questioning suspects casts one of the two investigating officers in the role of cruel, tough, uncompromising cop and the other offers hope of favors, speaks softly and pretends to be sympathetic, to keep suspect off balance and try to get information out of him or her.

muzzle loader—a weapon that is loaded from the opening at the tip of the gun, rather than at the breech.

mystery—a "homicide without witnesses or leads, with few if any clues."—Count, *Cop Talk*. The opposite of a **grounder**.

Nair bomb—a variation on the **flaming shit bomb**, this police harassment trick uses the canned chemical for women to remove unwanted hair from legs, etc. as a nasty item to drop on the cops.

narc—narcotics officer.

neighborhood store—smalltime drug selling operation.

nembies—nembutal (a barbiturate); pentobarbital.

new boot—see **boots**.

Newfoundland test to become a cop—a Newfoundlander goes in for the test to become a cop. "Three questions," they say: "Name two days of the week that begin with T." "Today and tomorrow," he answers. "O. K., what's one and one?" "Eleven." ....."O....K....Who killed Jesus Christ?" At which he stalls, "Ummm....er.....could I have some time?" "Sure," they say, "come back tomorrow." Walking down the street, he sees a friend, who asks, "How'd it go?" "Fine, fine," he says; "I answered the first two questions easily, and they sent me out on me first murder case!"

in a **New York minute**—a very short time, as in "they'll steal the hubcaps off your car in a New York minute, if you park it there."

N. H. I.—"No Human Involved," a cynical way to tag the murder or other case as not very important, the opposite of a **red ball**. A similar item of cop slang to **misdemeanor murder,** as it rests on the assumption that blacks, Indians, etc., are not human.

nickel bag—$5 bag of drugs (obsolete? although it still appears for "five dollar bag of heroin in a Special Fraud Squad glossary of abbreviations and jargon, New York City of approximately 1980 vintage).

nicknames—police, among themselves, do have nicknames, usually derived from specific incidents in the person's work history, but they avoid using them when in the presence of anyone not a fellow police officer. They also avoid using real names in such situations, and numbers are confusing, as there are too many different numbers around. In describing a situation, the DFW Airport SWAT team uses the term **Eagles** for their own. See also **canaries, crows.**

niggers in action—phrase used by prejudiced cops when black people cause trouble, derived from the standard radio call for trouble, e.g. "burglars in action."

night stick justice—from the idea that the police car function as a whole justice system by using force, i.e. "old school cops doing their job."—McCarthy, *Vice Cop.*

nine-one-one—"Dial 9-1-1, Make a Cop Come," T-shirt slogan, bumper-sticker. The emergency number on North American telephone systems.

no-badge—derogatory name for private police, security guard. "You can't do shit to me, you no-badge motherfucker!" See also **Mickey Mouse security guard, rent-a-cop, sweetchuck.**

no-nail—detonating device for explosives, to blow doors open, in **SWAT** team attacks.

nose candy—cocaine.

N. R. C. calls—Nobody Really Cares calls, expressing cops' feeling about many calls they get, that nobody cares one way or another. False alarms, vagrants loitering, etc.—Joseph Wambaugh, *Fugitive Nights*, p. 95.

number—marijuana cigarette.

numbers racket—an illegal lottery usually based on sporting events, especially horse racing.

observation sales—a routine arrest procedure situation among NYPD narcotics officers, involving an "observation post," **the op**, and someone in it is **doing ops** "on a rooftop or in a vacant apartment to watch a **set**, or drug operation, and transmit information to the **catch car**, the unmarked van used to pick up the **perps**. The "set" might be a lone teen-ager standing on a corner with one pocket full of crack and another full of cash. Or it might be an organization of such intricate subterfuge—with **lookouts, managers, moneymen, steerers** (to guide customers) and **pitchers** (for the hand-to-hand transactions."—Laffey.

O. D.—overdose of narcotics.

Old Sparky—ironically jovial name for the electric chair.—Leonard, *Maximum Bob.*

one-eight-seven—from 1-8-7, LA police slang from the code for homicide. Used in the rap music of Gangsta Rappers and others.

onion—a tear gas bomb.

on the pad—same as **on the take**, referring to a policeman who takes bribes. "Pads" were bribe schemes in the New York Police Department before the 1970 Knapp Commission allegedly cleaned up the department.

on the pink—"training to become a traffic-collision investigator. Officers must pass a 'pink test'—a term whose origins are unknown—to continue on the beat. 'My partner's **on the pink**, but she's got her test next week.'"—"L. A. Speak," *Los Angeles Times Magazine*, March 26, 1995.

one-time—(n.) "a warning given to a suspect when the officer doesn't have enough evidence to justify an immediate arrest. 'Hey, fool, that's **one-time**: I don't want you hanging around here anymore.'"—"L. A. Speak," *Los Angeles Times Magazine*, March 26, 1995.

arrested him **on looks alone**—recurring phrase to describe a cop's acting on instinct, sometimes with good results. The police knack for spotting criminals by their looks or suspicious demeanor. "Large fires attract every nut in the city. You could arrest a lot of these people on looks alone."—Fletcher, *Pure Cop*, p. 48. See also **attitude arrest,** being arrested for being an **asshole in the nighttime.** See also **firesetter, Fireman's Friend, hinky, spider sense.**

on top of a bomb—bomb squad expression for act of approaching a bomb to dismantle it.—Fletcher, *Pure Cop*, p. 1. See also **go up on a bomb.**

oo-wop—a gun. See also **bis, biscuit, jammie.**

Op, ops—see **observation sales.**

Operation Garden Plot—according to Thomas E. Ricks in January 1993 *Atlantic,* Marines' phrase for the military deployment in Los Angeles to restore order during the riots after cops lost control following the acquittal of the policemen involved in the Rodney King beating.

organ trophy—after the murder, a part of the victim which the killer removes and keeps.

the out—theoretical device/excuse which detective subtly allued to when interrogating murder suspect which enables suspect to confess or start talking, while in his mind justifying or lessening the seriousness of his crime or part in it. "Homicide detectives in Baltimore like to imagine a small, open window at the top of the long wall in the interrogation room. More to the point, they like to imagine their suspects imagining a small, open window at the top of the long wall. The open window is the escape hatch, the out. It is the perfect representation of what every suspect believes when he opens his mouth during an interrogation. Every last one sees himself coming up with the right combination of alibi and excuse. Every last one sees himself coming up with the right words, then crawling out the window to go home and sleep in his own bed."—Simon, *Homicide.*

"He came at you, right? You were scared. It was self-defense."
or "Maybe you didn't kill him, but you were there and saw who did. Tell
us who did."

outer perimeter—see **inner perimeter, kill zone.**

out-of-towners—easy victims of street crime, according to Stroud, *Close
Pursuit,* p. 208.

outside—slang code for "behavior not sanctioned by the rules, laws, or
guidelines for police conduct." "We're so far outside on this one it's not
even funny"—said by one cop to another after they had killed nine guys,
in the movie *Showdown in Little Tokyo.*

packing—carrying a weapon.

paddy wagon—police prisoner transport vehicle. Partridge attributes it to
the large number of Irishmen in the U.S who were policemen; or to the

large number of irish transported in them. **Black Mariah.** (Brit.)

paper pusher—person who deals counterfeit money. —Petievich, *The
Quality*

paper trail—refers to need for police to document all actions taken, in
paperwork, so that if questions arise later his or her action can be proven
and justified by a paper trail. Also, investigators' reality: subject's actions in
a) big cases such as white collar crimes, or b) missing persons cases, will be
documented by a findable paper trail which will lead to solid case against
suspect or in finding the missing person.

parrots—in **SWAT team** operations, a term used to identify persons who
are hostages but who may not be depended upon because of the
Stockholm syndrome.

pat-down search—police search for weapons on subject to ensure safety, no
consent needed, but limited to frisk of clothes for weapon-shaped object.

peanut butter crank—grainy, brown **speed** (amphetamine).

pedo—short for "pedophile," a person who preys sexually on underage victims.

the Peel—method of safe breaking in which burglar peels back metal sheet to expose bolt system or locking mechanism.

peeler—In Northern Ireland, term of insult hurled by Catholics at police, according to "Belfast: A City of Two Tales," Montréal *Gazette,* July 4, 1992. Cited thus in Partridge's 1937 *Dictionary of Slang and Unconventional English*, which traces its origin to Sir Robert Peel, Secretary for Ireland 1812–18. The more generally known term for police in the British Isles, **bobbies,** also comes from Sir Robert, this time from his first name. After he was Secretary for Ireland, in 1831, he founded the Special Constabulary, and thus became the founder of the modern police force. See also **rozzers,** and **Bow Street Runners.**

the Pepsi challenge—borrowed as a name for a Mexican police interrogation/torture technique where carbonated beverage, e. g. Pepsi, is shot up the nose of the suspect until it feels like his head is going to explode.—Joseph Wambaugh, *Fugitive Nights*, p. 312.

perp, perpetrator—suspect. One observer comments that unlike **assailant**, which tends to be used about black or hispanic suspects, this term tends to refer to "white guy implicated in or arrested for a crime." It has also been observed in use more in the U.S. Midwest and the East than in the South.

perp walk—a police-choreographed public unveiling of a prime suspect to the media, done for publicity, but somewhat unobtrusively, unless the **perp** is important, in which case it may be around the block, and known as **parading the perp.**—Philbin, p. 170

perpetrator immobilization patterning—a joke that convulses several of the television show NYPD Blue cops about an event in which one of them fires repeatedly at a suspect in a drug raid who is firing at him, missing him narrowly each time but miraculously escaping injury himself. "You shoot so close all around him that he doesn't dare to move." (March 14, 1994).

P I—private investigator, **dick, Dick Tracy.**

pick up a tail—start to be followed by another vehicle.

piece of the action—a portion of the profits from a criminal act or criminal trade.

pig—derogatory term for "police officer." Especially widespread during the 1960s. A prison guard in Los Angeles reports that during this time, he and his colleagues took to wearing a "P I G" pin which explained the letters as standing for "Pride, Integrity, Guts."

pig on a wheel—"motorcycle officer" (trucker's slang)—Roth, *The Writer's Complete Crime Reference Book.*

pigeon drop—a con game involving dropping a wallet or purse so that victim picks it up, and then is conned out of money.

pimp bar—a. k. a. "corrupter bar," a place where pimps hang out, do coke, and recruit girls for their stables.—McCarthy, *Vice Cop*, p. 183.

pimp's stable—the group of hookers at a pimp's disposal.

pinch—arrest (Chicago). See also **collar.**

pipe bomb—like the **Molotov cocktail,** a homemade bomb, using a pipe for compression of explosive. "The most common bomb out there today is the hand-ignited pipe bomb. Very simple to make—black powder—powders are very easy to obtain: take ordinary shotgun shell powder with plain ordinary what we call cannon fuse, which you can buy in any hobby shop, put it in a pipe, and you got one hell of a device."—Fletcher, **Pure Cop,** p. 22.

piped—Canadian prison guard's term for execution of an inmate by others, using a pipe over the head. "I knew that if we didn't keep an eye on this small, wild-eyed wraith, we could find him piped behind a garbage can."...A "pipe artist" is "someone who could walk up behind anyone of any size with a pipe or similar instrument, crush his skull, ditch the weapon, then have a big lunch and a long, dreamless afternoon nap."—Yates, **Line Screw**, defining a "heavy."

pissing on us—lying, telling bullshit story. "Don't piss up my leg." "I think he's pissing all over us and calling it rain."

pitcher—a key person in an **observation sale.**

Plain Jane—unmarked police car.—Poteet & Poteet, *Car & Motorcycle Slang,* iUniverse, 2000. See also **cop 'stang, cruiser, auto banalisé, weight watcher.**

plain view search—whatever a policeman can observe while legally detaining a suspect.

plant—to place evidence of a crime, such as drugs or a weapon on or near someone to cast suspicion on them. See **frame.**

player—"I'm not a pimp; I'm a player."—*Rough Justice.* According to Marcus Laffey, quoting a NYPD drug squad officer, a "player" is a dealer in drugs. Also referred to as a "bad actor."

plea bargain—a verb and a noun describing a negotiated agreement between one of several suspects and the prosecutor to trade testimony against others for a lower sentence, lesser charge, etc.

pocketbook drop—a con game.—*Rough Justice,* p. 121.

pocket prints—signs that a man is carrying a fat wallet or a gun. Stroud, *Close Pursuit,* p. 100

police work is 90% boredom and 10% sheer terror—maxim about the nature of police work.

Ponzi schemes—see **pyramid schemes.** "One of the earliest known examples of a pyramid scheme appeared in 1920 in Boston MA" and was created by "Charles Ponzi, an Italian immigrant and financial wizard. Mr. Ponzi promised investors they would double their original investment. Although Ponzi claimed to be producing profits by taking advantage of the varying currency exchange rates, in different parts of the world, he was suspected of actually taking money from one investor to pay off another. Eventually he was convicted and of the $15 million he took in, $8 million was unaccounted for."—Swanson, *Criminal Investigation,* p. 498.

poor man's cocaine—sobutyl nitrite. A cheaper drug with effects similar to cocaine but perhaps more dangerous to the user. Nash.

pop—1. inject (drugs) under the skin.
    2. arrest someone.
    3. murder someone.

a **popo**—an instance of "pissing off a police officer." An arrest/investigative rationale. See **ALJ, attitude arrest.**

poppers—street name for a dose of amyl nitrate, a heart stimulant.

Poppy Loves—elderly Jewish males, seen as easy victims to rob.—Stroud, *Close Pursuit,* p. 98.

population—"in population", among prison guards, means "among the inmates" of the prison.—Yates, *Line Screw.*

posse—a group of men deputized to act for the state, from "posse comitatus," "the power of the state to call upon all able-bodied men to assist in apprehending law violators."—Robbins, *The Texas Peace Officer Basic Training Course.* Jamaican gang groups, in recent years, have been known as "posse gangs."

potsy—NYPD slang for "policeman's breast shield" or badge. Also **tin.**

pour pattern—"not many fires start at floor level, so pour patterns are an indication that gasoline or other fire accelerant was used at fire, indicating arson."—Fletcher, *Pure Cop,* p. 53. See also **burn pattern, accelerant.**

powders her nose—snorts coke. In a bar: "Where's Lisa?" "Oh, she went to the head, to powder her nose."

power shift—common name for shift of veteran officers scheduled at high crime times or in areas to overlap regular beat shifts.

the **press-up**—in **SWAT team** assaults, just before they **breech** the door and charge in, they do the **press-up**, which consists of lining up in a row, each with finger on trigger, gun up by face (keeping it in close), and do a round of finger signals, the **double tap**, signaling each other that each one is ready.

probable cause—what a cop needs to make an arrest, perhaps 20% of the way toward a certainty that a suspect has committed an offense. To obtain a conviction, there must be "proof beyond a reasonable doubt," more like 90%. See **rap** and **ride.**

problem—universal insider police force word for any incident, often used on the intercom radio for conciseness and to avoid giving away the exact nature of the difficulty. "We've got a problem behind Building 3" tends to be a signal that backup is needed.

professional torch—an arsonist for hire.

priors—previous convictions.

profiling—detective method of creating a psychological and social portrait of a multiple murderer, based on crime scene details and **M.O.**—Philbin, p. 181.

the **Pry**—creating a gap large enough so that a jimmy type tool can pry open safe door. See also **blasting, burning, drilling, the Rip, manipulation.** An alternative to these procedures is the **Carry Off.**

public service homicide—"when somebody kills the scoundrel on the block, nobody minds." People do not help the police to solve the case. The phrase has a kind of humour: it parodies the "official, big-word identification of kinds of crime.

pucker factor, pucker power—degree to which a situation is able to scare the shit out of you, scares you so bad your butt cheeks clench. "You cannot become complacent. The pucker power is always there. Every device you go up on is a bomb."—Connie Fletcher, *Pure Cop*, p. 2,3.

the **Pull method**—of safecracking, the "drag" or "come along" method used on metals which resist punching. Use of wheel-puller tool to pull lock spindle out and gain entry. See also the **peel.**

pull an L. A.—to treat a suspect with excessive force, also known as to **Rodney King him, tee off on him, went off on him, went to town on him.**

pulling a train—refers to a woman's taking on a number of men sexually; gang rape or not, it is "training" or initiation into some criminal motorcycle gangs.

the Punch—method of safe breaking involving removal of combination dial and then using a drift or punch knocking the lock spindle through the locking case, thus forcing the locking mechanism out of position. Also called **drifting** or **knob-knocking**.

purple microdot—form of LSD.

pusher—drug peddler.

pussy wagon—fancy car such as a Corvette, which attracts women.

pyramid schemes—illegal games in which riches are promised and not delivered. Also known as **chain referral schemes** and **Ponzi schemes**. "A marketing program by which people buy the right to sell others a specified product. The promoters select a product, such as household items, cosmetics, or safety devices, and sell large inventories to distributors with the added incentive of permitting the distributor to sell new distributorships. The real profit is earned primarily by recruiters developing new recruits, who develop even more recruits. In all of this activity, there is little or no real concern given to direct sale of products or services to the public. Consumer distribution therefore becomes a sham, and acts merely as a cloak of respectability."—Swanson, *Criminal Investigation*, p. 498. Essentially another form of Ponzi scheme still prevalent today in various forms. Basically involves making money by buying into a pyramid chain at the bottom and moving up the pyramid to recoup investment by inducing at least two other people buy into the pyramid below you. Only once you reach the top of the pyramid do you profit. Each new investor gives half his buy-in investment to his recruiter and the other half to the person at the top of the pyramid, who leaves the top after earning sixteen times his earlier investment. Early investors in a pyramid game have a better chance of profiting, but eventually people will lose because "an infinite number of investors is needed to fill the chart from the bottom up."—p. 500.

quick change scam—see **fast change scam, con game**.

quick push—an easy victim.

quitter—suicide.

went rabbit—tried to jump wall and escape the prison.—from Federal Correctional Institution tour, Bastrop, TX.

rabbited—escaped.—Los Angeles prison guard talk. Also hit the wire.

"He looks like he could have a little rabbit [or 'rabbit blood'] in him," means "he looks as if he might try to escape."

rabbit trail—a diversion, deflection, or "false trail" from the path to a clear and dependable answer to the question "Who did it?"—David Boatright, Texas Department of Public Safety lawyer, Austin TX.

racket—"NYPD slang for a private police party."—Carsten Stroud, *Close Pursuit.* See also choir practice.

racketeers—organized criminals. Compare with vice lords.

rank and file—the ordinary policeman. Line police officer. Uniform.

rap—a charge. See ride.

rap sheet—list of arrests and convictions on given suspect.

R. A. T.—Radio Aided Tracking. High-tech strategy whereby a tiny transmitter is put into the money stolen from a bank so that the police in pursuit may find it and make arrests.

rat—as a verb, to inform. To squeal, be a stool pigeon.

ratboy—NYPD slang for "a man skilled in testing the strength of various illegal drugs."—Stroud, *Close Pursuit*, p. 335.

Rats and mice—for dice.

Rat Squad—division of a police force assigned to internal investigation, by reputation chosen because they have busted other cops and thus are ostracized, not trusted by their fellow officers, and in need of protection. From NYPD Blue, "That's how you end up on the Rat Squad." Officlally known as Internal Affairs.

Rat Trap—"A police anti-theft car, known as the Rat Trap, was stolen from Bath Lane, Newcastle upon Tyne. The engine of the white E-registered Ford Sierra, which has caught 31 thieves in the past 18 months, should have died after only 20 yards and hidden door and window locks trapped the thieves inside. A police spokesman said, 'There was a malfunction.'"—London *Observer*, 11 October 1992.

reach out—pull some strings. When one cop contacts another cop from another department or detail and either enlists him for help in a case or tries to affect a case being worked on. "I'll reach out to someone I know in Vice and see if they can help with this thing." "I know a guy over at the 2-5; I'll reach out to him and see how big a case they got on your brother." Not precisely the same thing as "to reach" a witness, which can mean, "to intimidate."

reaching out—shorthand term for a cop's "making an approach to another law officer to try to persuade him to drop charges against a suspect who assaulted him, but in extenuating circumstances." NYPD Blue, March 14, 1994. It may also be used to refer to trying to influence someone's choice in the presence of a discretionary alternative, or to get assistance, by appealing to their cameraderie as a police officer.

real victim—police expression for victim who was a good citizen, who didn't deserve or precipitate the crime against him. See Simon, *Homicide*, p. 515.)

red ball cases—"murders that matter—homicide cases that leave a city agitated and become media flashpoints requiring serious in-depth police investigation—from David Simon's *Homicide*. See also **whodunits, dunkers.** "Red Balls" are "murders that matter." "In this town, a detective lives or dies on the holy-shit cases that make it clear who runs the city and what they want from their police department. Majors, colonels, and deputy commissioners who never uttered a word when bodies were falling all over Lexington Terrace in the summer drug war of '86 are now leaning over the shoulder of a detective sergeant, checking the fine print." This term comes from railway slang, where a "red ball freight" was a fast, top priority, get-out-of-its-way train. The opposite is a **misdemeanor murder,** or may be referred to as **N. H. I.**

reds, red birds, red bullets, red devils—a barbiturate, Seconal.

red flag—a method of injecting heroin, in which the needle is inserted and the bulb allowed to expand until blood shows in the works."—Stroud, *Close Pursuit,* p. 335.

red light district—aarea where prostitutes work.

Rent-a-Cop, Rent-a-Pig—derogatory names for security guard, private police. See also **Mickey Mouse security guard, no-badge, sweetchuck.**

repo man—short for "repossession man," a person who retrieves cars from people who haven't made their installment payments on the loan.

revolving door of justice—the reality of our court and prison system is that early release, paroles, and the complications of the trial process mean that lots of criminals are free to come and go quite regularly. Awareness of this fact burns out cops.—Austin *Chronicle*, Dec. 18, 1992, p. 14.

rice—cop slang for maggots on a dead body.—Joseph Wambaugh, *Fugitive Nights.*

rice and beans squad—Arson, Explosion Squad, together with FBI agents who were involved in the efforts to solve the FALN [Fuerzas Armadas de

Liberacion Nacional Puertoriquena] during the mid-1970s, "because there were so many Hispanics involved."—Count, *Cop Talk.*

ride—the ride "downtown" or to the police station, as in the proverb "You might be able to beat the rap, but you can't beat the ride." This may seem to be a sarcastic and ironic way of telling a suspect that even though the case may not make it to court or a guilty finding, the crook will still be punished by being brought to the police station and likely spending the night there. To a media person hostile to the police, it suggests the brutal ride implied in **screen test for the LAPD**, or worse. But to a law enforcement insider, it simply expresses the difference between the degree of **probable cause** required to arrest someone (20% or so) and that required to convict (90% or so), "proof beyond a reasonable doubt." From David M. Boatright, instructor, Texas Peace Officer Laws class, Austin TX Community College, 1993.

riding shotgun—in a police cruiser, the person in the front passenger seat is literally "riding shotgun" as the shotgun is next to him and his hands are free while the driver operates the vehicle.

righteous—legitimate, justified, defensible, as in "a righteous shooting," said of an incident in which a cop fires his weapon within the confines of the law, e.g. in self-defense or in defense of another.—NYPD Blue 05/11/94. From black talk, originally from Southern religious talk.

riot cuffs—see **flex cuffs**.

rip—in NYPD, a "fine imposed for infraction of police regulations."— Anon., "Police Cant......oh yes they can!" *Spring 3100* (October 1958).

the Rip—uses crude force to penetrate the metal face of the safe. Often accomplished with axe to bottom of safe (not effective against burglar-resistant safes).

R M P—Radio Motor Patrol Car/ NYPD Squad Car. See **cruiser**.

road kill—body killed by a motor vehicle.

road rage—dangerous loss of temper behind the wheel, sometimes leading to violence or accident. See also **'roid rage.**

rocks—street name for crack cocaine.

rodeos—years in prison, in Texas, since they used to have a yearly rodeo in penitentiary. The number of rodeos a convicted person would attend would coincide with the number of years he had to serve. "He got ten rodeos."—from David M. Boatright's Texas Peace Officer Laws class, Austin Community College TX.

Rodney King him—to treat a suspect with excessive brutal force.

rogue cop—a lone wolf policeman, who disdains and doesn't follow his force's rules.

'roid rage—used to describe the condition of a steroid user who loses control of temper and becomes violent.

'roids—slang short term for steroids.

rollin' stolens—stolen cars apprehended while they are still running. (San Antonio, Texas) Compare **full float.**

roll over, roll them—cause criminal to turn informant. David McGee, U. S. federal prosecutor in Florida, explaining why Americans caught and imprisoned Allan Ross, alleged drug kingpin from Montréal before the Canadians did, said, "We have stiffer penalties, so that we can make the lower-downs roll over on the higher-ups." See also **turn, flip.**

rookie rubber—among **scooter trash**, i.e. motorcycle policemen, pieces of split garden or heater hose, fitted onto the side rails of the motorcycle during training, so that "when they fall over, it doesn't skin up the motorcycle."—Dean Thompson, DFW Airport SWAT team sergeant.

a **room for the night**—arrested, locked up. "Listen buddy unless you want a room for the night, you better get the hell out of here."

rozzers—Cockney for **coppers**, probably by association with Sir Robert Peel, who founded the British police in the early 18th century. Still in use by the Civic Guard in Ireland. See **peelers, bobbies**.

rub out—to kill, in older usage especially. Perhaps partly replaced by the synonymous, and more contemporary, **whack out** or **whack**.

ruffles—handcuffs, in England, 18th and early 19th century.—Grose, *1811 Dictionary of the Vulgar Tongue*.

rule one etc.—in the detective's lexicon, rule 9a: "to a jury, any doubt is reasonable." Rule 9b: "the better the case, the worse the jury." Rule 9c: "a good man is hard to find but twelve of them, gathered together in one place, is a miracle."—from Simon, *Homicide*, p. 451. In a death investigation, rule one is "everyone lies." Corollaries: a. "Murderers lie because they have to.

  b. "Witnesses and other participants lie because they think they have to."

  c. Everyone else lies for the sheer joy of it, and to uphold a general principle that under no circumstances do you provide accurate information to a cop. (p. 34)

rule two—in the Homicide lexicon: The victim is killed once, but a crime scene can be murdered a thousand times.

run a paper—obtain and execute a search warrant.—Mark Earhart, DFW SWAT team (motorcycle).

running hot—police car running with lights and sirens to an emergency.

safe house—a witness protection residence, to protect them from retaliation.

sandwich job—a whitewash police hearing after a wrongful death, police brutality, etc. charge.—from Petevich, *Money Men.* See also **shit sandwich review.**

Saturday Night Special—a cheap street gun, usually .22 or .32 calibre.

scooter trash—affectionate term for motorcycle cops. (TX)

screen test for the Police Department—suspect is handcuffed and put into the back seat of the police cruiser, but without fastening his seat belt. Then the driver takes the car through a series of fast twisting turns and sudden stops and starts, and you know the screen between the front and back seats? The screen test! (we heard this definition attributed to the LAPD long before Rodney King was on videotape).

screw—prison guard.

scrip—prescription for drugs, from an old word for "money." Also, currency in prison.

script writer—sympathetic doctor or prescription forger. Also known as "Dr. Feelgood."

secretaries with guns—according to Simon, *Homicide*, the way women cops are generally viewed by older "old school" cops. **Dickless Tracy.** But see also **Jane Wayne Syndrome, Dirty Harriet Syndrome.**

Seekers—preferred name for themselves by a group of New Jersey **bounty hunters**, who try to dignify their job by reading philosophy and "seeing their job in metaphysical terms."—Patrice O'Shaughnessy, "Bounty hunters 1994: Rambo learns philosophy," Montréal *Gazette* (January 30, 1994).

sell back—occurs when a victim is approached by criminals, receivers, or fences who offer the return of the stolen merchandise for a small percentage of its replacement value.

sell it to the insurance company—slang for "burn one's own house or business to collect the insurance on it."—Fletcher, *Pure Cop,* p. 66.

serial killer—a killer who commits several murders, usually following a pattern, i. e. stalking nurses, prostitutes, etc.

Serpico—has become a generic name for an overly clean, by the book cop, deriving from the New York detective who exposed widespread corruption in the New York Police Department during the 1960s and 70s. "I'm sorry, I insist on paying full price for my meal." "O.K., Serpico."

set—see **observation sales.**

sexual asphyxiation—one of the more interesting forms of suicide, in which subject hangs self while masturbating, supposedly to enhance stimulation and bring self close to the ultimate orgasm, as described, e. g. in William Burroughs *Naked Lunch*. *Criminal Investigation*, p. 373.

shading the duke—NYPD phrase for "covering the fingers during a pickpocket effort."—Anon., "Police Cant......oh yes they can!" *Spring 3100* (October 1958).

a good **shake**—cop slang for a car "likely to be worth checking."—from Joseph Wambaugh's *The Onion Field*.

shakedown—the use of police power to demand cash, bribe, favors.

shank—a knife.—from Federal Correctional Institution, Bastrop TX, tour. Another word than "knife" is needed because of the variety of ingenuity used in the making of these objects by desperate inmates: "Toothbrush knives, made from one or more disposable razor blades heated and sunk into the non-bristle side of the toothbrush, and string wrapped around the handle to guarantee a good grip; shanks, made from metal spoons, but also made of pieces of glass with strips of sheet wrapped around for a handle....."—Yates, *Line Screw*.

shanked—stabbing (common prison term). Any hard object obtained is sharpened into a "shank," which is then used as a weapon.—from G. Petevich, *Money Men*.

shine—"NYPD slang for a useless bureaucrat, from the shine on the seat of his pants."—Carsten Stroud, *Close Pursuit*, p. 336.

shine him on—"cut him loose"—Joseph Wambaugh, *The Onion Field*.

shitcanned—case thrown out, arrest not pursued.—Stroud, *Close Pursuit*, p. 163.

shit sandwich review—an internal police department review of performance which results in critical evaluations being surrounded ("sandwiched") by compliments. See also **sandwich job**.—from Petievich, *Money Men*.

shitstorm—serious pressure, complaints, and even potential demotions, etc., from chain of command as in when **red ball case** is not solved. Shit flows downhill. See **fecal gravity**.

shoo-fly—"superior officer assigned to inspectional duty"—Special Fraud Squad glossary of abbreviations and jargon, New York City. Much feared because he's looking for cops breaking the rules.

shooting gallery—locale of drug use, especially injectable drugs like heroin, cocaine, etc.

shoot up—to inject drugs intravenously.

shopper—car thieves, **boosters**, who cruise parking lots looking for cars to break into and steal. (TX).

shopping job—private police/investigator name for loss prevention work where they often pose as a shopper and try to spot employee theft.—Joseph Wambaugh, *Fugitive Nights,* p. 106.

short-eyes—"a man who has a sexual fixation on young girls."—Carsten Stroud, *Close Pursuit.*

shoulder surfing—"sneaking a look at someone,s ATM (automatic teller machine) information [especially the PIN, or personal identification number, as it is entered) in order to rob the account later."—Philbin, p. 197.

Signal X—used on the radio to say "female," as for example, when an officer alone is transporting a woman whose car has broken down to her house, and he wants it on the record just how long she was in the car: "Transporting a signal x from Oak and Main"; "delivered signal x to 1234 Smith Street at 5:03 p.m."

sing—to talk, confess, or **rat out** a fellow partner in crime. See also **give up**.

sing operas—to give police a lot of information about a criminal operation. From "Lords of the Mafia," aired on PBS March 2, 2000. This term may be behind the naming of the lead characters in the HBO Mob series "The Sopranos."

sit on—to sit on a suspect or drug house, to "maintain surveillance on"...

sitting duck—police name for a stolen car found abandoned on the street, which is quite common when kids steal a car for a **joy ride**, then strip it and leave it on the street. Also called a "duck."—Joseph Wambaugh, *The New Centurions*. See also **hot roller.**

six pack of witnesses—bringing in a lot of witnesses into court can be good or bad for a case. Too many witnesses can bore or confuse the jury.

skel—NYPD for homeless person. Lowlife street drunk/druggie. Short for "skeleton." A very old phrase.—McCarthy, *Vice Cop*, p. 41. "She looked miserably down and out, a 'skel,' as the cops would say. I think the term was short for human skeleton."—*Rough Justice*.

skimming—underreporting hard to track income (such as gambling house profits) to the Internal Revenue Service.

skin popping—injecting drugs under the skin.

skip tracer—P. I. who locates missing persons, usually through **paper trail** and telephone work. See **chase paper.**

sledge man—guy who knocks the door down in police raid.

sleeper hold—a neck hold which causes person to quickly lose consciousness, more precisely known as "carotid control technique." Involves "applying pressure to each side of the neck and causes a substantial reduction in the supply of blood to the brain." Some RCMP say they were not formally trained in the use of this hold; some older Mounties said they had not had refresher courses since they were recruits, in an investigation into the question of whether excessive force was used in certain arrests in 1991. (Montréal *Gazette*, July 21, 1992). Mostly obsolete, due to potential for lawsuits, in the UA, police defense technique in which officer grabs suspect from behind with a choke hold to the neck, applying pressure to the carotid artery, thereby cutting off oxygen flow to the head until the suspect loses consciousness. If applied incorrectly or for too long, it can kill the suspect. See "doing the **funky chicken**," **choke hold.**

slicks—"Vietnam combat term for Medevac chopper; used in the NYPD to imply the arrival of a bunch of **shines** whose job it is to cover up a departmental mistake and protect the bosses at One Police Plaza."— Carsten Stroud, *Close Pursuit.*

slim jim—a thin piece of metal used to open locked car doors.

smack—heroin.

Smokey—local or state police.

smoking gun—when the suspect is caught literally with the weapon in hand, just after committing the crime. See **slam dunk.** This use is to be distinguished from the more well-known sense of the phrase, where it merely means "an appearance of what may be evidence of serious trouble...."

SMT—Special Missions Team. See **SWAT team.**

smurfs—drug-cartel employee who handles money. "The husband and wife were 'smurfs,' a type of drug-money launderer in prolific use by the Cali cartel....A husband-and-wife smurfing team will travel from bank to bank, posing as strangers, each depositing some of the cartel's money under a false name, or converting it into cashier's checks, always in sums under ten thousand dollars."—Fredric Dannen, "Colombian Gold: Annals of Justice," *New Yorker*, Aug. 15, 1994. See also **structuring.** **Smurfing** is the verb form.

snake pit—place in school where illegal activity occurs.

snappers—amphetamine drugs, **speed.**

snaps—street alternative to violence, way to vent frustration and not lose face without fighting: verbal comeuppances. "Your mother....."—from MTV Free Your Mind series, 04/11/94.

snitch—sing like a canary, sing, spill his guts. Confess or tell on others.

snoop—to spy on, investigate.

snuff film—movie in which a person is actually killed on film.

sock-hop—in a **blanket party,** in a Canadian prison, a beating administered by a bar of soap in a sock, which makes the victim feel battered for days but leaves no marks and doesn't skin the knuckles of the attacker.—Yates, *Line Screw.*

soup jobs—jobs where **blasting,** explosives, are used to attack a safe.

Spanish handkerchief switch—a con game.—*Rough Justice,* p. 121.

Special K—on the coast, Veterinary drug Kedamine, an animal tranquilizer used in seduction: "it brings 'em up, like cocaine, but then it relaxes 'em on the way down."—Count, *Cop Talk.*

speedball—injecting stimulant and depressant at once. Originally heroin and cocaine. Also called a **whizz bang.**

speed freak—substance abuser, habitual user of amphetamines.

spooks—ordinary cop term for CIA and Federal agents, because they are not identifiable by uniform.

sports bourbon—bourbon and urine, actual drink served in a New York gay club. To be safe, cops working undercover always order beer in a bottle. from *Vice Cop,*

spud gun—homemade explosive device that fires potatoes, from a pipe, at high speeds....a type of **zip gun**. From Austin TX *American-Statesman,* Aug. 6, 1993.

squattting—living in an abandoned building belonging to someone else.

squeal—to **rat**, to inform on associates in crime. See **sing, stool pigeon.**

squirrel—a **snitch**, an **informer**. "Guy might be a fucking squirrel if he did time in that place [Vacaville, a hospital prison]."—Joseph Wambaugh, *The Onion Field.*

squirrel sheriff—a game warden, to other law enforcement officials. Also called a **sparrow cop.**

stake-out—old, perennial term for a police operation involving covert surveillance of a location.

stand-up guy/gal—a witness who will not be intimidated, who will not change his or her story under pressure, who will not **roll over** on you. Also, a cop who will **back up** his fellow officers.

stealth entry—quiet entry, involving the **press-up**, the **double tap, hand signals**.—from DFW Airport SWAT team members.

step—invade a person's space to assault them, black street slang. "Don't step."—from hiphop/rap music. Paris.

step on—dilution of drug, typically heroin or cocaine, with some other substance. "How many times you gonna step on it?" The **cut**.

the **steps and the string**—early 18th century jocular way to describe execution of criminals by hanging, from Daniel Defoe's *Moll Flanders:* "some of my worst Comrades, who are out of the Way of doing me Harm, having gone out of the World by the Steps and the String, as I often expected to go."

sting—as memorialized in the movie by that name, a staged fake police raid in order to take money from other criminals or customers who are doing something illegal or disreputable enough that they will flee rather than fight or complain to the real cops.

Stockholm syndrome, stockholming—hostages sympathizing with hostage-taker. From a bank robbery in Stockholm, Sweden, where hostages sympathized so much with hostage takers that they would not testify against them and later married them.—Fletcher, *Pure Cop*, p. 232.

stool pigeon, stoolie, stool—a suspect who informs on others as a way of trying to get a lighter sentence, for cash or revenge, or to escape being charged. A **squealer, canary**. Eric Partridge identifies the origin of this very old expression (from 1880) as from bird-hunting, where pigeons were tied to wooden frames ("stools") to attract wild birds within range of gunners.

strawman purchase—"a gun can be bought by a qualified buyer on behalf of an ineligible buyer: this is known as a strawman purchase and is prohibited by federal law."—"Brady Law," *Austin American Statesman*, Feb. 27, 1994.

the **street**—"is the generic term given to the world of predators and victims outside the police station. Anyone working a case, from street gang specialists to vice cops to hostage negotiators to evidence technicians to bomb and arson and major accident investigators, work the street to solve it."—Fletcher, *Pure Cop*, p. 268.

street justice—when police deal out punishment where courts fail to, or when they feel courts will fail to or are not necessary.

street smart—tough cop or criminal familiar with ways of the street.

streetwalker—prostitute.

the **stressor**—"an anxiety-filled event that triggers a murder."—Carsten Stroud, *Close Pursuit*. See also **double whammy**.

stringer—suicide by hanging, in prison. Yates, *Line Screw.*

structuring—"breaking down large sums [of drug money] into small pieces to avoid having to file a C.T.R." {currency transaction report, which requires personal information about the customer to be reported to federal authorities}. A technique of **smurfs**.—Fredric Dannen, "Colombian Gold: Annals of Justice," *New Yorker*, Aug. 15, 1994.

stun gun—weapon that delivers an electric shock which temporarily incapacitates suspect. See also **tazer**.

sugar daddy—pimp and/or drug dealer. **Candyman.**

sugar shittalk—pimp conning a girl to work for him uses this, sweet talk, promises and lies. From Black talk.—McCarthy, *Vice Cop.*

suicide by cop—may occur when a suicidal person points an unloaded or fake gun at cops to force them to kill him. "Suicide by cop. Somebody's suicidal—maybe he's just found out he has brain cancer, but he doesn't have the balls to commit suicide himself. So he tries to do it by pointing an unloaded gun at a cop. That's what's really going on with a lot of our barricaded, depressed subjects. They want to commit suicide by cop. This is common."—Fletcher, *Pure Cop*, p. 228.

suit—1. "young, educated officer likely to advance to headquarters."—Roth, *The Writer's Complete Crime Reference Book*.

2. among DFW Airport SWAT team officers, this term means "a straight detective."

3. Also, according to Philbin, "a boss who has no value, an 'empty suit.'" P. 212.

suitcased—"a method of concealing capsules of a drug inside a condom or balloon inserted in the anus or the vagina."—Carsten Stroud, *Close Pursuit*, p. 337.

summer heatwave theory of inner-city mortality—an explanation of the increase in violence in hot summer (and full moon). See Simon, *Homicide*, p. 516. See also **full moon theory.**

Superman syndrome—see **John Wayne Syndrome.**

superspook—overtrained, underpracticed government agent (CIA) weirdo. There is a longstanding deep-seated resentment of Feds amongst city cops.—from Archer Mayor, *Open Season*.

swag—stolen money. See Elmore Leonard, *Swag*.

swallowed the .38 caliber aspirin—when a world-weary cop takes his own life (by placing his service revolver in his mouth and pulling the trigger) thereby ending his suffering.—Joseph Wambaugh, *Fugitive Nights*, p. 153. **Swallow his gun. Eat your .38.**

SWAT team—elite Special Weapons and Tactics squad, present in all big city police departments, comprised of highly trained paramilitary officers used mainly in hostage type situations. Also called **SMT** (Special Missions Team), in Austin TX, and in some cities **TAC squad** (Tactical Squad). **Containment officers. HBT team.**

sweetchuck—a derogatory name for a security guard or private police. "Don't be a sweetchuck!"—from nerdy small recruit character in the Police Academy movies, also used at Fanueil Hall Marketplace security force, Boston. See also **Mickey Mouse security guard, rent-a-cop, door-shakers, no-badge.**

swinging the ram—knocking in door with police battering ram in a bust.—from police tape, Cops in Pittsburgh.

syndicate book—a mafia run bookie operation. Nash.

syringe banditry—"Muggers are finding that a syringe full of blood and the words 'I'm HIV positive, give me your money or I'll inject you' are more effective than a gun or knife." Report from Lisbon, in *The European,* 1993.

TAC squad—Tactical Squad. See **SWAT team.**

take a flying fuck at a rolling doughnut—terms of endearment among police at the donut shop. Police and donuts have a long rich tradition, perhaps from the days when the only thing open late at night were donut shops.

take a walk—to go free, to get off scot free, to get "cut loose" by the cops.

take 'em down—verbal signal to take action, stop and arrest, e.g. a stolen car that one is following.

You can **talk the talk but can you walk the walk?**—street question—can you back up your tough talk with actual toughness and fighting ability?

tar—heroin from Mexico (brown).

tazer—a form of **stun gun.**

ten card—"officer's force record card."—Roth, *The Writer's Complete Crime Reference Book.*

ten code—military/police radio code system. **Code 3** is "lights and sirens," an emergency. **Code 4** is "problem cleared, no need for further assistance."

testilying—giving false testimony under oath in hope it will lead to conviction of a person you believe to be guilty. Also known as **white perjury,** on the analogy of "white lies."—from interview with James D. McNamara, former police chief of Kansas City and San Jose, in *Harpers* (August, 1997). Still in use in California in 1999: "You'd have to be awfully naïve to think a police officer never lies. There is a term in the criminal justice system, 'testilying' that pretty well covers that"—assistant public defender Kalunian, in "In L.A., a land outside the law," *National Post* (Thursday, November 25, 1999).

THC—tetrahydracannabinol, the active ingredient of marijuana. Can be purified resin extract or synthetic product.

theory of the case—a hypothetical reconstruction of the crime or of the line of investigation of the crime, to be tested in the interrogation or search for evidence.

thin blue line—honorific, romantic image of the police, as it refers to the idea that between the tidal waves of crime and the lives of ordinary citizens there is only, for protection, the "thin blue line" of police officers.

the third degree—phrase heard in movies and TV programs to denote police brutality or at least extreme pressure in interrogation. According to Charles Earle Funk's *Heavens to Betsy! & Other Curious Sayings*, it comes originally from the Masons, in which it refers to "the third and final stage of proficiency demanded of one who seeks to become a Master Mason....elaborate and severe, but never injurious."

three card monte—common street con game.

throwaways—clothes robbery suspects ditch after fleeing scene to confuse police description and avoid apprehension.—Stroud, *Close Pursuit,* p. 99.

throwdown, throwdown weapon, throwdown gun—

1. a spare gun (or knife) allegedly carried by police to throw down surreptitiously during a confrontation with a suspect, to justify shooting him and exonerate the police during the hearing that follows. Obviously an illegal act. Timbuk 3, a music group of the 1990s, has a song about a throwdown gun. Also known as a **drop gun.**

2. as referring to a cop, a **throwdown** is a rookie officer or an unreliable one, someone you "use if you have to," but not for normal duty.

throw phone, field phone—a heavy duty plastic military phone in canvas bag, used by hostage negotiators to make contact with hostage taker or barricaded individual.—Fletcher, *Pure Cop,* p. 235. "Throw" refers to how the phone is passed to the hostage taker.

thunder stick—a 12-gauge shotgun (FBI term).—from "Annals of Crime: A Violent Act," *New Yorker*, June 15, 1992.

timbit—In Québec, among the Quebec Provincial Police, in French, an informal meeting at a coffee or donut shop is known as "un timbit." The term comes from a doughnut sold by the Tim Horton coffee chain, called a "timbit."—from Mitchell Herf.

time—prison term. "You did the crime. Now do the time." "You want to play; you have to pay." From a Chicago veteran cop: "ghetto saying: 'if you can't do the time, don't do the crime.'"

tin—police badge, ordinary cop. As contrasted with **gold**, a ranking officer or detective's badge.

token suckers, token sucking—"Up in the three-four precinct we've got a lot of kids who are into token-sucking, and they're always hitting up the same fuckin' turnstiles. Every morning they're in the subway ten, maybe twenty times and then they come back for more at night. And what they do ios, they slip a folded piece of paper into the token slot so the token won't go through into the token box. After a passenger loses a token and walks away, the kids come back, suck it out of the slot, and sell it for a buck on the street....They put their mouth on the token slot and suck. That's why it's called stuff'n'suck."—Heilbroner, *Rough Justice.*

toot—cocaine, aka **white lady, sleep, ice.**

torch—arsonist.

tossed—"searched," in the New York Police Department. Especially when drug dealers search an undercover cop trying to make a buy, to see if s/he's a cop.—Count, *Cop Talk.*

tracks—old drug users' term for needle marks on arms, legs, scars from repeated injections. Also called **turkey trots.**

—also, a "contract," as om "I got a track to kill him."—Susanna Moore, *In The Cut*.

trafficker—a person in the business of supplying drugs.

traffic stop—officer pulls car over after observing a moving violation. Dangerous because you never know exactly who you are stopping, and thus officer must treat every stop as a potentially lethal encounter.

trapdoor scab—scab on junkie used to stick needle under to hide fresh needle marks from the cops.—Joseph Wambaugh, *Fugitive Nights*, p. 34,35.

to **trap off**—to plea-bargain.—Susanna Moore, *In the Cut*.

trailer—sign of accelerant at a fire site, because the fire runs in a line following the accelerant when gasoline or other combustible is used to help it spread. Arson investigator's term.—Fletcher, *Pure Cop*, p. 52.

tricotage—Québec French police term for "weaving in and out of traffic on the freeway without using your turn signals, at high speed." Means "knitting", and is also used in hockey slang for "stickhandling" (see *Hockey Talk)*.

trip—take LSD. See also **drop acid**.

tune up—New York City cop slang for beating uncooperative witness/suspect up - working them over. See **attitude adjustment, the mechanic.**—from CNN newscast 10/06/93

turf war—inner city gang clash over geographical lines of criminal activity control.

turkey necker—a ghoulish observer of a traffic accident or police action, who ties up traffic and access to a crime scene.—Austin, Texas. See **ambulance chaser.**

turkey trots—see **tracks**.

turn—get a criminal to aid police in undercover operations against his former partners in crime, or testify against them.

turned to stone—used to describe a witness expected to testify who suddenly mysteriously forgot all he ever knew or formerly remembered about the case, presumably because of threatened reprisals from associates who stood to lose a lot by his testimony. Possibly a case of **eyefuck**. Certainly a case where the witness has **rolled over** on you.

turnkey—prison guard, a **screw**.

24/24 rule—"phrase referring to the last 24 hours of a murder victim's life and the first 24 hours after the body is discovered, which are the most important hours in an investigation."—"L.A. Speak," *Los Angeles Times Magazine* (June 13, 1995).

Two—"a black person, from the code used for racial categories on police reports (One: Caucasian; Two: black; Three: Hispanic.)"—Susanna Moore, *In the Cut.*

Two Golden Rules of the Mafia—1) Don't rat on your friends, and 2) Always keep your mouth shut.—from the movie Goodfellas.

Two-wheel Smokey—"motorcycle officer" (truckers' slang)—Roth, *The Writer's Complete Crime Reference Book.*

Unabomber—infamous serial bomber who terrorized the universities and company executives, especially in computer and airline manufacturing firms across the U.S. The word is made up of the first syllable of "university," and the "a" stands for "across the U.S. Police charged estranged loner Ted Kazinsky with the crimes, a series of bombing incidents which killed three and injured dozens.

uncle—one who deals in stolen goods. Also called a **fence**.

uniform—a uniformed policeman.

Unwritten Police Code of Silence—"Tell the same story and keep your mouth shut about other officers' indiscretions." Notice similarity to **Two Golden Rules of the Mafia.**

vaccinated—executed.—from Boatright, Texas Peace Officer Laws class, Austin Community College, TX.

vampires—cops who work late tours, like the "graveyard shifts," which actually see less crime than the most active 4 p.m. to midnight ones.

Vegas bankroll—see **Jewish bankroll, gypsy bankroll.**

verbal judo—"skillful use of language by police officers to defuse tense situations, says George Thompson. For a reported $2,200 (U.S.) a day the former cop/English professor is showing New York police that well-chosen words are better than harsh language or a whack with a nightstick."—Toronto *Globe and Mail* "Word Watch" (Sept. 7, 1995).

vics—victims, easy targets on street.

vice lords—powerful criminals. Compare with **racketeers.**

vig—from "vigorish," an old slang term for the high interest that loan sharks charge on loans.

wacky tobaccky—marijuana.

wake-up call—see **attitude adjustment**. Police using force or the threat of force to bring an unruly or confused individual back to reality.

walk—when arrested person gets to leave without facing charges. As in, "you talk, you walk. Otherwise, you're going down the river."

walk by—criminal threat to shoot someone. "Man, I'll do a walk by up in here." Heard in the movie "Great White Hype."

walking tall—From the movie of this name, a cop or man armed, on the move, and knocking down anyone who challenges or gets in his way.

walk the beat—see **beat.**

walk the line—gang initiation ritual in which "potential gang members have to 'walk the line,' a form of initiation in which a recruit walks through a group of gang members and is beaten."—Austin *American-Statesman,* Sun. September 6, 1992. Another initation requirement is that the recruit prove his worth at stealing cars.

war story—off-duty police recounting interesting experience from the street.

washing—evasive driving by a perpetrator under chase to 'lose the tail,' i. e. escape from the surveillance vehicle or vehicles. "The Colombian couriers keep their eyes glued to their rearview mirrors, make unexpected stops in the middle of streets, suddenly accelerate to dangerous speeds, jump several lanes of traffic, and practice a technique known as 'washing'—taking an absurdly indirect route from A to B."—Fredric Dannen, "Colombian Gold: Annals of Justice," *New Yorker*, Aug. 15, 1994.

wasp—a prostitute infected with Venereal Disease or AIDS. Coined perhaps because the insect has its stinger in its tail. Nash.

waterboy—a boxer who can be bribed or coerced into losing for gambling purposes. De Sola.

water sports—"perverted" sex act involving urinating or defecating on partner.

wearing a wire—said of a person, whether undercover or informant, who is fitted with a **body bug** for electronic surveillance/recording of conversations with criminal suspect.

weed—marijuana.

weight watcher—highway department vehicle to maintain surveillance on commercial trucks to ensure they do not travel overloaded.—Poteet and Poteet, *Car & Motorcycle Slang*, iUniverse, 2000. See also **cop 'stang, Plain Jane, cruiser.**

welfare queen /king—persons who are adept at defrauding welfare programs by using alias's.

wet-brain—an alcoholic inmate, in Canadian prison guard slang.—Yates, *Line Screw.*

wetwork—killing close up, face to face—Stroud, *Close Pursuit*, p. 210.

whacked him—killed him. From Hill Street Blues.

the **what you mean we, kemosabe look**—surprised look which says "I don't know what you're thinking about and even if I do, I don't, and won't **back you up.** You're on your own." *Homicide,* p. 415 .

wheeling a driver—"at an accident investigation, being able to prove that a specific person was driving a vehicle."—Robbins, et al, *The Texas Peace Officer Basic Training Course.*

white collar crime—"an illegal act of series of illegal acts committed by nonphysical means and by concealment or guile, to obtain money or property, to avoid the payment or loss of money or property, to avoid the payment or loss of property, or to obtain business or personal advantage."—Herbert Edelhertz, U. S. Department of Justice, in *Criminal Investigation*, 1970, p. 497.

white line fever—an adaptation of the traditional trucker's phrase for highway hypnosis, in cop slang usually means driving while high on cocaine, maybe overdosed, at high speed and with great nervous energy.

white perjury—telling untruths under oath, like "white lies," to convict someone you believe to be guilty. Also known as **testilying.**

white shield man—"a new detective who has not received his gold shield."—Special Fraud Squad glossary of abbreviations and jargon, New

York City. E. W. Count identifies "white shield" as the NYPD term for the (actually silver-coloured) detective badge. The gold shield represents a level of experience so that one is said to have **got made** when one receives it.

whizzbang—see **speedball.**

whodunits—homicide cases that are difficult to solve, requiring hard and skilled work from detectives; genuine mysteries. See the opposite: **dunkers.**—from David Simon's *Homicide.*

whoretel—motel or hotel frequented by whores and their clients. Nash.

wilding—gang members on the rampage, seeking victims to rape, rob and murder.

window pane—small piece of cellophane with LSD on it.

wire man—a wiretap specialist. See **bugs.**

wiseguy—a **made man** (i.e. fully accepted member) in the mob. See Nicholas Pillegi's novel of that name (1985). The term appeared as early as 1915 for "a small-time criminal" in a Kelillah (Jewish Community researchers') report on New York City's Jewish Lower East Side—from Robert Lacey, *Little Man—Meyer Lansky and the Gangster Life* (New York: Little, Brown, 1981).

Wolf—criminal especially pickpocket who operates alone. Also for detective. Short for **Lone Wolf.**

wolf packing—gang activity, especially mugging.

wood shampoo—a beating by police clubs.

word up—pay attention, "listen up." A street phrase.

working in the field, fieldwork—street work as opposed to desk job/paperwork.

works—equipment for injecting drugs.

xerox machine polygraph ploy—when detectives con dumb suspect into thinking a photocopy machine or other office machine can detect lies; done in order to elicit a confession. "Not long ago several veteran homicide detectives in Detroit were publicly upbraided and disciplined by their susperiors for using the office Xerox machine as a polygraph device. It seems that the detectives, when confronted with a statement of dubious veracity, would sometimes adjourn to the xerox room and load three sheets of paper into the feeder. "Truth," said the first; "truth," said the second; "Lie" said the third. Then the suspect would be led into the room and told to put his hand against the side of the machine. Two detectives would ask the man's name, listen to the answer, then hit the "Copy" button. "Truth." "And where do you live?" "Truth." "And did you or did you not kill 'Tater, shooting him down like a dog in the 1200 block of North Durham street?" "Lie." "Well, well, you lying motherfucker."—from David Simon's *Homicide,* p. 204.

Yakusa—the Japanese Mafia.

yegg—"a safe burglar."—Special Fraud Squad glossary of abbreviations and jargon, New York City. This is a very old bit of police/underworld slang.

yellow jackets—nembutal, barbiturate.

Yen shee—ashes of opium.

a **yo**—male gang or street kid. A **yoette** is a female gang or street person.

you're on your own—police higher-up expression to line officers, stating that if they do something not sanctioned by the department, the department will not back them at all, and that they will have to defend themselves against any legal actions taken against them. "If you shoot a suspect without shouting a verbal command to comply like 'Stop. Police!' or 'Drop the weapon' first, you're on your own.

yumyums—drugs found in medecine cabinet which are often taken by youths. Nash

zen—LSD.

zing—"departmental complaint."—Special Fraud Squad glossary of abbreviations and jargon, New York City.

zinger—"a summons; also a complaint by a Superior given to a police officer."—Special Fraud Squad glossary of abbreviations and jargon, New York City.

zip gun—homemade projectile weapon, any one of a number of types. See **spud gun.**

zips—crime family Sicilians imported as enforcers, perhaps because they "zip right back" to Sicily.—Count, *Cop Talk.*

BIBLIOGRAPHY

Anon., "Police Cant......oh yes they can!" *Spring 3100* (October 1958).

Anderson, Elijah. *A Place on the Corner.* Chicago: University of Chicago Press, 1978.

Baker, Mark. *Cops.* New York: Pocket, 1985.

Breo, Dennis L. and William J. Martin. *The Crime of the Century: Richard Speck and the Murder of Eight Student Nurses.* Bantam, 1993.

Buckley, Christopher. *Wet Work.* New York: St. Martin's, 1990.

Caunitz, William J. *Black Sand.* New York: Bantam, 1990.
　　　　　　　　One Police Plaza. New York: Bantam, 1990.

Corkum, Hugh. *On Both Sides of the Law.* Hantsport, NS: Lancelot, 1989.

Count, E. W. *Cop Talk: True Detective Stories from the NYPD.* Interviews with intro. by William J. Caunitz. (New York: Pocket, 1994.

De Sola, Ralph *Crime Dictionary.* New York: Facts on File, 1982.

Fletcher, Connie. *Pure Cop.* New York: St. Martin's, 1992.

Heilbroner, David. *Rough Justice.* New York: Dell, 1991.

Kelly, Bill, and Dolph le Moult. *Street Dance.* New York: Charter, 1987.

Edward Kirkman, "Wary of Perps & Shooflies, Cops Talk in Code," New York *Daily News* (November 12, 1974).

Laffey, Marcus. "Inside Dope," *New Yorker* (February 1, 1999), pp. 29-32.

McCarthy, Bill and Mike Mallone. *Vice Cop.* New York: William Morrow and Co., 1991.

McClure. James *Cop World.* New York: Pantheon, 1984.

Moore, Susanna. *In the Cut.* (New York: Onyx-Penguin, 1996).

Muir, William Ker Jr. *Police: Streetcorner Politicians.* Chicago: University of Chicago Press, 1977.

Nash, Jay Robert *Dictionary of Crime: Criminal Justice, Criminology and Law Enforcement.* New York: Paragon House, 1992.

Parkhurst, William. *True Detectives* New York: Jove, 1992.

Petievich, Gerald. *To Live and Die in L. A.* New York: Pocket, 1989.
  To Die in Beverly Hills. New York: Signet, 1989.
  The Quality of the Informant. New York: Pocket, 1990.
  Shakedown. New York: Pocket, 1988.
  One-Shot Deal. New York: Signet, 1981.

Philbin, Tom. *Cop Speak: the Lingo of Law Enforcement and Crime.* New York: Wiley, 1996.

Pistone. *Donnie Brasco.* New York: Signet, 1987.

Polsky, Ned. *Hustlers, Beats, and Others.* Chicago: University of Chicago Press, 1985.

Poppa, Terrence E. *Drug Lord.* New York: Demand, 1998.

Rachlin, Harvey *The Making of a Detective.* New York: Dell Publishing, 1995

Robbins, Ray K., Larry D. Nichols, Donald B. Harrelson, *The Texas Peace Officer Basic Training Course.* (Berkeley: McCutchan, 1990).

Roth, Martin. *The Writer's Complete Crime Reference Book* (Cincinnati, OH: Writer's Digest Books, 1990).

Simon, David. *Homicide.* Boston: Houghton Mifflin, 1991.

Special Fraud Squad (New York City) Glossary of Abbreviations and Jargon Used by the Department and its Clientele, September 14, 1974.

Stroud, Carsten. *Close Pursuit: A week in the Life of a NYPD Homicide Cop.* New York: Viking, 1987.

Swanson, Charles R. *Criminal Investigation.* New York: Random House, 1984.

Wambaugh, Joseph. *The Onion Field.* New York: Dell, 1974.
> *The Choir Boys.* New York: Futura, 1981.
> *Fugitive Nights* New York: Bantam, 1993.
> *The New Centurions.* Boston: Atlantic Monthly Press, 1970.
> *Lines and Shadows.* New York: Bantam, 1984.

Wozencraft, Kim. *Rush.* New York: Ivy, 1990.
Yates, J. Michael. *Line Screw.* Toronto: McClelland and Stewart, 1993.

Thanks to David Boatright, Texas Department of Public Safety lawyer and former Austin City policeman; Sgt. Curtis W. Gray, Chicago Police Crime Laboratory; David Michael Logsdon, San Antonio Police Department; Sgt. Dean Thompson, Dallas/Fort Worth Airport SWAT team.

Authors Lewis J. Poteet and Aaron C. Poteet, father and son, also wrote Hockey Talk, a dictionary of hockey slang. Lewis has written or co-authored four other slang word-and phrase-books; he taught English for 32 years at Concordia University in Montreal and in winter 2000, was adjunct instructor in English at Austin (TX) Community College. Aaron holds a bachelor degree in Criminal Justice from Northeastern University in Boston. As a sometimes wayward youth, he walked the city streets at night as neighbourhood patrol, Guardian Angel even vigilante. His near obsession with the street led to work in the most thankless profession known to man : Law enforcement. (and he loved almost every minute of it.) Working first as a Special Police Officer in downtown Boston for the better part of a decade then serving briefly with the Austin Police Department. He now works in the private sector as a field collector for a large corporation.

Michael Condon is a tattoo artist and freelance illustrator living in Austin, Texas. When he's not drawing, he can be found on stage singing and playing guitar for his band, the Flametrick Subs.

The manuscript to date draws on spoken and printed sources from Canada, Boston, Chicago, Texas, New York, and California and reaches back into old English word-books for police slang. It is a lively assemblage of the word-and phrase lexicon of the criminal justice speech community, containing clues to the pride, the corruption, the violence, the brotherhood, and the challenges of this profession.

APPENDIX
POLICE SLANG: AN OVERVIEW

he do the police in different voices—original title of T. S. Eliot's poem The Waste Land

As long ago as 1964, David Maurer, in *Whiz Mob* 1955 ("Epilogue"), wrote "The police—once a loose occupational subculture—are now turning into something that may be more sinister; under pressures, from the dominant culture and criminal element, many large police departments seem, in self-defense, to be tightening their subculture into a force that might some day give us the police state." He was disturbed by "the tendency in many big-cities" for the police, "driven by frustrations with citizens groups, economic factors, political organizations, the courts, etc., to reinforce their own occupational subculture and strengthen their control over the dominant culture."

One of the best ways to make stronger and also to examine closely a subculture is through language, particularly slang. Key to identity, revealing of culture and psychology, slang never lies.

And whether Maurer was prophetic about what police were becoming, and thus what they are now, the immense popularity of true crime writing and even true crime fiction show, as Alex Ross has written in the *New Yorker*, that "we have a need for the sight of life and death as for salt. We wage-slaves live continually in incompletion and inexplicability; we strain for a sight of stars and mud."

There is no better vantage point from which to see the stars and mud of human life, the best and the worst, than that of the police.

Cop talk reveals diverse origins and increasingly a great deal of (especially technical) commonality. It is different in some ways, especially historically, in Britain, Canada, and the United States. There are even words and phrases used more in the American Northeast, South, Southwest, and California, respectively.

It also shows the qualities of police culture, which is made up of the psychology of the men and women who serve in blue—the pride, the shame of corruption and violence, fear and contempt, cynicism and a mordant wit laced with black humor.

To gather this material, we have had access to a diversity of sources, which I will describe briefly.

The language patterns of the slang of police follow most of the ways of word and phrase-formation that other contemporary slangs do—shortening, using rhyme and acronyms, and some sensible reasons for the creation and use of police nicknames that echo that of gang leaders and members. And some of the items reveal very succinctly some law enforcement techniques that may surprise you.

In all, cop talk is an index to police cultures.

I. British, Canadian, and American regional differences

It is easy to find generalizations about alleged major differences in police cultures. Arthur Fleming, of Harvard, in 1962 claimed that the West had "order without law" and the East "law without order." Another, related belief is the accepted idea that Canada is made up of peaceable people and the United States of quarrelsome and violent ones based on the fact that the law came first to the Canadian West, whereas in the U.S. the outlaws got there first. In yet another, a SWAT team member at Dallas-Fort Worth Airport suggested (and not he alone) that the main police problem in the Northeastern U.S. was corruption, as compared with the Southwest's problem with police brutality. British police are supposed to be mannerly, as are Canadian. These words and phrases help to test these theories, which of course reach far beyond the individual and are full of exceptions.

Police in the Western world started in England, with the Bow Street Runners, named for the location in London where, in the early 18th century, organized social control of the modern variety was first attempted. Also during the 1700s, British Prime Minister Sir Robert Peel created a "national" force, lending to the language the familiar terms "bobby" and "peelers." In fact, a cockney version of his name, "rozzers," is still in use in Northern Ireland, where the survival also of "peelers" suggests the long resentment and primitive anger on both sides which lasted far into the twentieth century, and in fact still continues. We include also a few terms which give the flavor of that early work: "Beilby's (a form of the word 'bailiff') ball" was the spectacular, familiar, and immensely popular scene of a hanging. It was also known jocularly, in Daniel Defoe's early 18th century novel *Moll Flanders* as "the steps and the string."

But lest we think that the British are still stuck in the past, a couple of recent items show how international police tricks have become. What was dubbed "an alien sting" was a clever and very successful strategic police ploy to nab people who had illegal scanners to listen in on their communications. (They put out the disinformation that an alien craft had landed in a particular place, and some of the scanner-owners showed up there to be nabbed.) It is like one used in the U. S. and elsewhere whereby mailing notices of prizes to people wanted for as minor an offence as a stack of unpaid parking tickets brought them in for arrest in large numbers. Another British device, a car called "the Rat Trap," didn't work so well: engineered to tempt thieves, then stall and lock them in, it was stolen. However, the generally conservative nature of British policing is hinted at by their calling a "baton" what everyone else knows as a "billy club." And their continued use of this minimal equipment does remind that American police were also unarmed in the early 1800s, in imitation of the mother culture.

"Flatfoot," a term still in use in the U.S., according to the *Dictionary of American Regional English* (1991), seems to have originated in England, where it was applied to the battalion company in the Foot Guards (Hotten, *The Slang Dictionary*, 1859). Of course, foot patrolmen in the U.S. walked a lot, too; but "gumshoe," a related term for what Hotten calls "the lower classes" of police, seems not to have been used in England, though H. L. Mencken in *The American Language* (1937) found it in use a lot in the 'States. And where did "on the lam" come from? Lighter, in the remarkable recent *Historical Dictionary of American Slang* traces it to a Pinkerton detective, and ultimately to the language of pickpockets ("let the man go," they'd say, once they had made their move), but Gerald Cohen, who has studied slang at the University of Missouri (where the enormous Tamony Collection of underworld slang is stored), traces it to Britain, to "costermongers" or sellers from carts, and to a gypsy word "nammou," "to depart, especially furtively." He also thinks that "vamoose" may have been involved (*Comments on Etymology* 1997).

The globalization brought by myriad advances in communications and other technologies have of course been major in impact on police talk. In fact, many crimes either take place or are pursued and sometimes solved in what one aviation expert has called "globalocalities," as when a U. S. airplane, registered in Canada, made in several countries, flown by a Mexican crew, has an incident over the Pacific. So it is also when police forces collaborate, on fingerprints or descriptions and so forth, across the world. So also when a scholar from Canada's Simon Fraser University in Vancouver quits academia to use his expertise at assembling and studying demographic patterns to solve serial rapist or murder cases in places far from Canada. A "bomb dog" is familiar the English-speaking world over, as is also the "Stockholm Syndrome." One recent collection of police terminology, Tom Philbin's *Cop Speak* (1996) traces "bull," widely known as a derogatory term for a big, tough policeman, to Spanish gypsy slang, where a "bul" is an officer.

But what of those sweeping general statements about Canada and the U. S., and also of different regions in the U. S., which offer views of the differences in police cultures in those places? If the American Northeast is characterized as having an excess of police corruption, as compared with a brutal cop South, is it not because violence is the recourse when a police officer does not know the community? In New York, as in Montreal, I have often thought that close collaboration between cop and criminal grew out of a strategy of increased knowledge, containment, and perhaps control. If the American Northeast is so prevailingly corrupt in its police work, why has New Orleans been called "the most corrupt cop city in the U. S."? New York has suffered several embarrassing and tragic police errors resulting in the shooting of innocent people, but California cop slang is replete with terms for police violence: "to do a Rodney King on someone" has spread far beyond the place of its videotaped origin, and into another example of police cynicism: "first we treat him like a King, then we read him the 'menu' (the Miranda warning—"you have the right to remain silent….")." Los Angeles Police Department has been said to have "kill parties," to celebrate the death of a leading gang member. New York Internal Affairs Department distinguishes between "grass eaters," cops on the take in a small way, and "meat eaters," more greedy corrupt ones, but California contributed "black and white fever," to describe what someone has who runs from the cops, and one of the most poignant descriptions of someone dying on the street comes from there, too: he is, they say, "circling the gutter." Of course, too, in California, a "strawberry" is a prostitute who trades sex for drugs, rather than money, and a streetwalking prostitute is a "pavement princess," or a "sidewalk hostess."

It's been said that the police badge is known on the East Coast as a "button," but on the West as a "buzzer." In both Canada and the South and Southwestern U. S. it is said that a "blanket party" in a prison may be either inmates throwing a blanket over the victim to make it easier to beat him up, or police doing it. "Perp," widely known since the advent of the TV show NYPD Blue, has spread, but apparently not to the South, mainly to the midwest and the northeast. "Fuzz," a very old derogatory term for police, is both U. S. and Canadian in use, but its origin is obscure. It has been said that it referred to "Feds," making it U. S. originally; but it has also been described as an insulting term for any young policeman in Victorian days when older cops wore beards and moustaches. We include at least one French-Canadian term, "auto banalise," (banalized or neutered car), which is a Quebec term for what Americans know as a "Plain Jane," or unmarked police car. And aren't Montreal cops as brutal as anyone?* One of the original terms we found, "the screen test for the LAPD," has to my certain knowledge been used in Montreal, and sometimes for offenders who had unpaid parking tickets. (Look it up: it is a mean trick, even in a hockey town like Montreal, but attributing it to LA gives it a clever twist, because that's where Hollywood is).

To verify with exactness some of the answers to these questions, one would need to assemble and compare some statistics, 1. the crimes of violence count, say, between LA and Washington DC; 2. the solution rate in Atlanta and Chicago; 3. the overall crime statistics in any significant pair of cities in different regions.

Taylor Buckner, Professor of Sociology at Concordia University in Montreal, who wrote his PhD thesis in 1967 at Berkeley on "The Police: The Culture of a Social Control Agency," served as liaison between the university administration and the protesters sitting in at Sir George Williams disastrous 1970 Computer Sit-In, has given some eloquent and detailed first-hand observations on his experience in Oakland:

There was a police term, "humbug," which referred to calls or complaints of little value (from a police point of view). Thus, "all there was tonight was humbug," means a bunch of drunks got arrested, a couple of routine family fights, and neighbours complaining about neighbours.

---

* See Jacquie Charlton 1997, reporting on Gaetan Rivest" *Le Juste Milieu*, which is a monthly tabloid reporting on "police harassment, conflict-of-interest scandals, corrupt cops, and questionable deaths involving police at various levels" in Montreal.

California did not fit into the violence-corruption spectrum at all. There was a little violence, a little corruption, but nothing like the violence I saw in Louisville, KY, nothing like the corruption in the Mafia dominated Eastern cities. One Eastern cop said to me, "How does it work if there is no Mafia?" If anything California cops were brutally efficient bureaucrats, often graduates of Viet Nam. As one said to me, "Why should I sink to his level by hitting him? I have the entire Criminal Code at my disposition. If I hit him he will be sore for a few days, if I charge him with everything I can think of he will be in jail thinking about it for years. ....."

The police don't deal with violence very often. They do deal with the disorganized, the stunned, and the voluntarily substance handicapped a lot. From my experience,. family fights, which recurred in the same families every Friday night were the largest part of the caseload. It led to a great deal of cynicism among police officers because there was little helpful they could do. In one instance my partner had been to "The Browns" many times. It was the lowest house I had ever been in, excrement and food smeared on the walls, urine in the enclosed porch, etc. The "Browns" called the police every Friday. They were deranged, drunk, and hostile.

When we left, after temporarily dealing with the immediate problem, my partner commented, "Things are looking up?"

I was appalled, and asked, "What?"

He said, "Didn't you hear there was mention of a gun?"

I said, "How is this 'looking up'?"

He said, "The next time we get called we may be able to take the body to the morgue, the killer to jail, and the kids to welfare, and we'll be through with them."

As you suggest, corruption may come from the police being "too understanding," violence may come from the alienated sense of being an "occupying army" in "enemy territory." When we went into an Oakland housing project to recover a stolen car, it was enemy territory, we routinely took five police cars, 10 officers, and were often stoned by gangs of "youths" who were bringing each other up. (from email correspondence)

Some terms are certainly American in origin and use. The acronym "goyakod"—which stands for "get off your ass and knock on doors," more politely known as "canvassing," is the door to door search in a "red ball" case when the police have no suspects or need more information from witnesses. Acronyms are a largely U.S.-military-promoted affliction of the age.

England's distinctive and local cop dialect includes "blagging," (robbing), a "blood-print," ("a print made by an attacker's finger, wet with his victim's blood. An excellent piece of evidence"—Scotland Yard Metropolitan Police glossary in Peter Laurie's 1970 *Scotland Yard,* Appendix Three), a "bustle-puncher," (someone who feels up—"caresses", according to the glossary, "ladies' bottoms in a dense crowd.") The politeness of the British police is suggested by the polite indirectness of "Coat, have you got a?" which is explained as "intimation of arrest." Understatement, characteristic of British speech, is in "over the side, to be," explained as "to be about one's own affairs, usually sexual, during time on duty."

We found in Victoria, only (not that it isn't perhaps used elsewhere) a complete list of the terms pimps use and cops know in Victoria, British Columbia, Canada: the "mains" are the primary girls controlled by the pimp; the "wifies" the "next rank of prostitutes," the "turnouts" "young girls recruited into the sex trade," the "kiddie stroll," ("a city block known for its younger flesh on display," and "leaving fees," or "money paid to a pimp when a girl leaves.")—Detective Mike Sikora as quoted in the Toronto *Globe and Mail* of March 1, 1999.

So, despite the unanswered or only partly answered questions I have raised, we may say that there is in fact considerable evidence in the slang that police cultures in different places do in fact differ in some important ways.

II. Police Culture and Psychology in the Slang

In turning to the hints in the language police use that suggest aspects of their psychology, we may as well link this part with the discussion of violence in the previous section. The entire concept of "hot pursuit," so recurrent in debates over police procedures, safety, and the law, is based on a law that itself derives from the psychology of the wolf and the dog, in which capture is all-important. But the slang contains items that may be classified more subtly.

Pride is foremost among a group of terms which refer to blue, the common colour of the police uniform: "blue flu," "blue wall (of silence)," "the thin blue line," and "Blue Knight," all of which are of course favourites among officers who are proud of what they are doing (or in some cases, ashamed, as in when the blue wall of silence protects someone who has made a bad mistake.) Some notable crime fighters have had their names memorialised in a sort of oral Hall of Fame by having their names made generic: a Serpico, the Eliot Ness Syndrome, and so forth. Someone who is too proud may be called "badge-heavy," especially a rookie who revels in the power of the "Masterbadge," as it is called when it is flashed to get a free meal. The pride of the law enforcement officer is considerable when they can take even "pig," the insult hurled at them by protesters in the 1960s, and turn it into an acronym for "pride, integrity, and guts," as some California prison guards did, putting it on a pin they wore.

But if pride is the good angel on one shoulder, a raft of terms record the instances of corruption and vigilantism among cops. To take bribes is to be "dirty," to be a "grass-eater" or a "meat-eater." A "Dirty Harry" is not above resorting to whatever he must to get the job done; a "Dirty Harriet" is the same, but with the added handicap of being a woman in an often traditionally misogynistic profession. A "drop gun" is a dirty trick, to justify a shooting of a suspect which may lead to exhaustive and potentially disastrous hearings. A civilian vigilante is a "Bernie," named for the well-known man in New York (Goetz) who took the law into his own hands. We have mentioned the impact of the Rodney King beating on the language, but the "green-stick fracture," as Spider Robinson (Sci-fi writer and columnist in Vancouver, BC, Canada), says, is in store for a man who gives his wife a black eye more than once. "Groin soccer" is a way to refer to physical abuse during an interrogation. And the police use of Mace gets rhyming slang: it is "spray and play."

Cops have to deal with the worst, as Taylor Buckner has said, and so the language reveals this grisly side of the subculture. One homicide squad made its trainees look through a "family album" featuring particularly graphic cases, to see if they can take it.

Cops are cynical, and because they have mixed feelings about what they have to see and sometimes do, they get witty to relieve the strain. A "mushroom" is an innocent bystander killed in a shootout, because they spring up and then disappear, their names unknown before and after, unlike a Dillinger or O.J. Prison guards, as Tom Philbin reports, call it "back gate parole" when an inmate escapes by dying before release. Cops in Texas and California speak of beatings as an "attitude adjustment," parodying the language of the new, educated cop. But some of the darker feelings are behind a routine LAPD radio salute at the beginning of a shift: LSMFT stood for "Let's Shoot a MotherFucker Tonight," especially vivid since "motherfucker" was a common insult hurled at them in the 'hood.

One Texas ex-cop and instructor in criminology told me that his colleagues would often say, "Let's put the habeas grabbus" on him, parodying the "habeas corpus" law which so often released improperly arrested suspects, arrested on too little probability and too little evidence. Cops do make mistakes. They call it, "putting the gun on the nun," or "putting a rope on the Pope."

Still, there is a prevailing feeling among police officers in the 'States that almost everybody out there is at least an asshole, if not a downright criminal. Some are clear: a range of terms, regionally distributed, refer to the killing of a really undesirable, difficult character in a community: a "misdemeanour murder," is one such; they talk of the "needs killing defense," and the "public service homicide."

Cop slang is rich in terms of contempt. "Perps" are "skels," meaning perhaps "skeletons," and even prosecutors, who work for the same side, are sometimes called "dumb ass" in parody of their title, District Attorney (DA). "Yos" are black suspects in Neil Simon's original book *Homicide*, though not in the TV series. Even minority officers, increasing in numbers in many metropolitan forces, have been called "black and blues."

Cop talk has a few phrases that hint at the inevitable fear they feel. "Suicide by cop," when someone wants to die but lacks the courage, and so does something which will bring out a firing police revolver, is dreaded by everyone. It leads to work for the "headhunter," defined as a member of the Internal Affairs Department who checks on officers' behavior, and also known as the "Procto Cop." A civilian review board, where they exist, has been said to be made up of "wimps and pimps" by disgruntled, over-worked, terrified officers. The worst of all is to take "the 38 calibre aspirin," or to "swallow your gun." But it happens.

In recent years more minority officers have been hired, and more women, and a new vocabulary, often euphemistic, has appeared. They're not "J.D.s" any more: they're "at-risk youth," or CHINS (Children in Need of Supervision.) One cynical Arizona cop said, exasperated, "I don't solve social problems: I make arrests." But when in Winnipeg a sex trade worker was killed, and the cops called it "lifestyle related," the public anger took the form of a play. "She took the low track," the new agers said.

III. Some Sources we used

Quite a lot of police slang has been widely spread in the 1990s by such popular shows as NYPD Blue, Homicide, and the Canadian Top Cops. We have tried to monitor and mine these shows. Some older terms came from older shows: a "Barney Fife" lasted from the Andy Griffith show to describe a downhome, small-town cop; and it led to a "Bubba Fife," which is less complimentary.

We talked with SWAT team members at Dallas-Fort Worth Airport, Jesse Dean Thompson and Mark Earhart, to whom we are grateful for their sharing their insights and talk. They mentioned a very interesting set of words which are helpful in a SWAT assault on a hostage-taking inci-dent: cops call the hostages "canaries," the fellow officers "eagles," the hostage-takers "crows," and those whose loyalty is uncertain, perhaps victims of the Stockholm Syndrome, "parrots." They also described the "press-up," a key tactic discussed further on under words that describe specific strategic moves. One of them said that in recounting personal history stories from police work, one never used real names or numbers, but nicknames, to conceal identity. I suspect that there is a mirror phenomenon among drug gangs, whom I am told always given nicknames to kingpins and important gang members so that they may not only stand out among members but not be so easily known to the police. Of course the media has made this hope vain in some cases, as Gottis and O J s and numerous other high-profile figures have been celebrated, become authors, and so forth.

We talked with a member of the San Antonio Police Department who passed along a copy of a fascinating small handbook, prepared for his colleagues who spoke no Spanish, giving the local vernacular of about 80% of the public in that city for "face down" ("bacabajo"), spread your cheeks, etc. (Only 20% of the force was Hispanic in 1995). (Serrato, 1992) They also mentioned that police groupies are known locally as "fender lizards," and the informant thought that was local, not even used as nearby as Houston.

We were kindly given a copy of the New York Police Department Special Fraud Squad list of Abbreviations and Jargon ("used by the department and its clientele.")

Some other sources of cop talk are criminal talk, and because the U. S. gives so much attention to black suspects in many places, some cops talk is derived from black speech. To "get up" is to spray your gang symbol all over the 'hood to mark control over the turf. A "righteous shoot" owes something to those old black preachers.

We have looked through many of the many books of true crime and true crime fiction—such works as Philbin's *Cop Speak*, Count's *Cop Talk* (a book of stories), and many memoirs by ex-cops and ex-police chiefs.

No dictionary is ever complete, and we invite readers who think of items not included to send them to the publisher to be forwarded to us. Or mail them to 51 7th Avenue., Roxboro, Quebec. H8Y 2W1.

III. Language Patterns in the Slang

The way words and phrases are formed, the shape they take, is discussed in good detail in Connie Eble's *College Slang 101* (Spectacle Lane Press, 1989) and in the introduction to J. E. Lighter's *Random House Historical Dictionary of American Slang* (1994). Among some of the word-formation processes they describe are several shown in this book: "tec" for detective is shortening, as is "got the bitch," which also rides on the double whammy of the shortening of "habitual" and the shock value of "bitch," which surely describes the feeling of someone who is declared to be a "habitual criminal." "Cop" itself is probably a shortened word-part; "perp" certainly is. There is alliteration, the repetition of initial sounds for added effect in "a bus and a boss," and ""bust balls." There are chains of parodic phrases: "hijacking," "skyjacking," "carjacking." What Lighter calls "connotational incongruity" (perhaps a big-word way to say "parody") is in "Habeas Grabbus" and "Masterbadge" for Mastercard. There is such rhyming slang (like Cockney) as "kick in the dick," (to subdue a perp), "swervin' Mervin," (a drunk on the road), "reveal the eel" and "Grand Opening" for flashers. There are deliberate oxymorons (phrases in which the parts should logically contradict each other, like "accidentally on purpose." I find none of the insertion of a word into a compound existing word, like "motherfuckingChrist," which Lighter finds a pure slang word-formation technique. But no doubt cops do it.

More work needs to be done on this aspect of this material.

IV. Terms that reveal Techniques

The language of cops is full of traces of and in some cases dramatic, surprising strategies and tricks they use. The homicide lexicon rule "24/24" means that for investigative success, the most important hours are the last 24 hours of the victim's life and the first 24 hours after the body is discovered. The "good-guy/bad-guy technique" is familiar in interrogation, and is also known as the "Mutt and Jeff routine." In SWAT team assaults, just before breaching the door, the cops line up in the "press-up," guns up at their faces and fingers on triggers, and without talking, they do the "double tap," to signal "all ready." LCC in such situations is "last cover and concealment." When a cop is told to "fade the heat," he is being told to "ride the trouble out and keep your job."

An arrest is a "cuff and stuff." "Probable cause," a legal term, is to cops a formula: you need 20% probability to make an arrest, said David Boatright in Austin, but 90% for "proof beyond a reasonable doubt" to obtain a conviction. And in one interesting story, I was told that one squad would pick a "color of the day" to signify the terrifying "cop in trouble" situation in code. But the most odd term of this sort we found was the "fruit machine," a device used by Canadian law enforcement back in the bad old days to pick out homosexuals, based on their optical and racial reactions when shown pornographic images, for example, of pedophilia.

The book has been a challenge to do. Enjoy.

Lewis J. Poteet
Roxboro, Quebec, Canada
May 13, 2000.

Sources cited.

Cassidy, Frederic G. *Dictionary of American Regional English.* Vol. 1. 1985 Cambridge, MA.: Belknap Press of Harvard University Press.

Charlton, Jacquie. "Reporto cop," *The Montreal Mirror.* (1997). November 13.

Cohen, Gerald. *Comments on Etymology*, Vol. 27, No. 1. 1997.

Count, E. W. *Cop Talk: True Detective Stories from the NYPD*. 1994. New York: Pocket Books.

Eble, Connie. *College Slang 101*. 1989. Georgetown, CT: Spectacle Lane Press.

Fleming, Arthur. Lecture at Harvard University. 1962.

Hotten, J. C. *The Slang Dictionary*. 1859. London: John Camden Hotten.

Laurie, Peter. *Scotland Yard: A Study of the Metropolitan Police*. 1970. New York: Holt, Rinehart and Winston.

Lighter, J. C. *The Random House Historical Dictionary of American Slang*. 1994. New York: Random House.

Maurer, David. *Whiz Mob*. 1955. Publications of the American Dialect Society.

Mencken, H. L. *The American Language*. 1937, 1963. New York: Alfred A. Knopf.

Philbin, Tom. *Cop Speak*. 1996. Toronto: John Wiley.

Roberts, David. "A real-life street drama turns tragic," Toronto *Globe and Mail*. 1998. (March 25).

Robinson, Spider. "When the Monsters Come: The Crazy Years," Toronto *Globe and Mail*. 1998. (March 2).

Ross, Alex. "The Shock of the True," *New Yorker*. 1996. (August 19, pp. 70-77).

Schmidt, Sarah. "Victoria deals with outbreak of teen prostitutes," Toronto *Globe and Mail*. 1999. (March 1).

Serrato, James. *Survival Spanish for Emergency Responders*. 1992. San Antonio TX: Streetwise Technologies.

Simon, David. *Homicide: A Year on the Killing Streets*. 1991. Boston: Houghton Mifflin.

Appendix II: Stories

1. The Walter Walk

We had a regular homeless person named Walter who we were constantly having to deal with. He was tall and ugly with lots of greasy black hair. Even sober, he scared the general public with his unkempt appearance and scowl. But his general demeanor darkened considerably when he'd been drinking, of course. He could be a pretty mean drunk and a real pain in the ass. Walter was notorious and infamous for his staggering drunk walk in which he always looked like he was just about to fall down but somehow rarely ever did. It was a sort of one-step-forward-two-steps-sideways gait that made him recognizable from blocks away with the naked eye. We called his patent stumble the "Walter Walk," and sometimes attributed it to other drunks we'd come across: "Man, that guy had the Walter Walk going on, didn't he?" or even to each other to bust balls, "Man, you sure tied one on last night! When you came out of the bars, after last call, you looked like old Walter on a bender….."

Anyway on one occasion we got a call that Walter was being disorderly in the central food court of Faneuil Hall Marketplace. One of my fellow officers arrived first and saw Walter stumbling along up ahead of him. He reported that Walter was in rare form, bouncing off counters and customers alike like a pinball. As he approached, Walter had reached the end of the building and staggered out through the open double doors, which led to several stone steps down to the street. The officer, whom I'll call Ed, realized that in the particularly inebriated state that Walter appeared to be

133

in, he might not notice the steps and was likely to fall. Ed hastened to catch up to Walter before he plummeted off the end steps.... Sure enough, just as he arrived behind the drunk, Walter teetered off the edge. Ed lunged to catch him, missing by a fraction, but catching his shirt, which pulled away as Walter nose-dived face first into the concrete ground, busting open his face.

To passersby it looked like he'd pushed Walter off the edge:

"Look, Mommy, that officer just threw that homeless man down the stairs."

Even on videotape the scene would have looked bad. Poor Ed looked like he'd lost it in front of a crowd of witnesses: caught with the proverbial smoking gun in hand. As a crowd of angry onlookers gathered, we tried to persuade them that he wouldn't do that to old Walter, as much as he'd like to at times. Like I said, Walter could be a real pain in the ass.

2. Busting Balls

One relatively slow Saturday night, Ed and I were patrolling the grounds, trying to pass the time. As we stood talking to one of the sausage cart vendors whom we knew pretty well, we cooked up a scheme. A call came over the radio about some trivial thing that didn't require our assistance. But the sausage vendor couldn't hear the particulars of the call over the din surrounding his stand. Often bored and desperate for some distraction, he and other merchants were always asking us about our work, grilling us for details about the calls we got. He wanted to know what was going on. So we started playing with him.

"Sounds like there's a big fight down by Cityside Bar," Ed said.

"Man, I'm sick of those guys, let them deal with it on their own," I said.

"Yeah," Ed said, "if we go down there, we'll just end up having to arrest somebody!"

Then we resumed small talk with each other....The vendor was shocked.

"Aren't you guys gonna go over there and help out ?" He protested.

We acted like we just didn't feel like dealing with it.

"Naw, I hate having to do all that paperwork!"

"Fuck that, we don't get paid enough to deal with that crap!"

The vendor had to serve a customer, and meanwhile our radios crackled with more insignificant crap.

"Sounds like someone pulled a knife over there..." We mentioned to pique his interest.

"You guys gotta get over there, man." The bewildered vendor pleaded with us.

We began a relaxed discourse on how unpleasant and bloody knife incidents were.

"Fuck that, I hate all that blood, nowadays you don't know what people could give you, bleeding on you and shit."

Next Eddie reached down and made it seem like he was turning his radio off. I acted like I did the same....

"Hey, you wanna go get a bite to eat? Man, my stomach's putting out an **APB** for food."

"Yeah, I'm starving. How 'bout pizza?"

"Sure."

We strolled off as the poor vendor protested and shook his head in disbelief.

3. Batting Practice

One night while on patrol with Ed, we saw what looked like a fight starting between two young males in the alley next to a flower/souvenir stand. As we approached, one of the assailants backed out of the fight, turned and ran right past us yelling "he's got a knife!" Sure enough the other combatant had what looked like a knife in his hand. He was blind with rage or bloodlust. I don't know, but it was like he didn't even see us, was going after the other guy. He ran right at Ed, who struck him with his nightstick in the upper leg and torso. We're both yelling, "Drop the knife!" "Drop it!" The guy isn't fazed by our series of commands or Ed's nightstick blows! I swing my nightstick at the knife hand and connect right on the wrist. Crack. His hand snaps open, and the knife pops out like a cassette tape coming out of a car stereo. I **de-knifed** him so to speak and the "knife" (which turned out to be a pair of scissors he found in the flower market) fell to the ground. The guy resists arrest, and we have to wrestle him to the ground as well. But before we can finish cuffing him, the other assailant comes in trying to kick the guy. So we're trying to keep him at bay while we finish handcuffing the struggling scissorman.

Finally, we get the guy cuffed, and Boston Police shows up. Well, our other assailant took off just before BPD arrived. He wanted no part of pressing charges or even being a witness; probably he had outstanding warrants. Anyway the cop gets out of his cruiser, and he knows the kid (a **townie**). We want to press charges on his attack on Ed, but the cop wouldn't hear it. He says he'll put the kid in for **PC /protective custody** (some time in the Police Jail to sleep it off). But what he really does is drive the kid over to the bridge back to Charlestown and let him off, we figure.

Anyway, I like to remember this incident even though the guy got off scot-free, because it's one of the few times I returned the favor for the many times Ed nailed someone with his nightstick who was about to suckerpunch me or kick me or whatever. Plus, for an incident involving a deadly weapon, this contact turned out surprisingly well: it was exciting, nobody got seriously hurt, and there was hardly any paperwork to fill out, to boot. Incidents with a knife involved are usually a lot messier than that.

4. Doing laundry

Once we got a call that one of our regular homeless guys, "Hughie," was loitering in one of the restaurants on the property. Hughie was an elderly eccentric homeless alcoholic whom we all knew pretty well from years of dealing with him. Hughie was famous around town for his expression "I'm not as young as I used to be," his hunched forward stance and for still being on the street even though he was damn near 90 years old. Still drinking after all these years. Someone once told me that these people have about a five year life expectancy once they hit the street. But Hughie was an exception, he'd been around as long as anyone could remember. He was a character, who was often good for a few laughs.

Anyway, on this particular occasion, when we arrived at the restaurant, we saw Hughie standing inside the patio area of the restaurant, which was closed for business but still open to walk through. As we approached Hughie, we found him standing over by the dishwasher, which was running. He seemed to be fiddling with the machine. As we walked up, I said, "Ok Hughie, let's move along, come on now, quit playing with that, it's not a toy,."

Hughie smiled. "I'm not playing with it," he said, opening the now finished dishwasher, he reached in and extracted something.

"I'm just doing my laundry," he said, holding two dripping socks and a pair of BVD underwear in his hands...

There was always some disgusting story circulating at work.

Another time one of our other homeless regulars walked into the very same restaurant during business hours with customers at the tables, "dropped trou," squatted, and dropped a load in the middle of the restaurant. For sheer gross-out effect, that was probably the worst. But we had plenty of other crazy restaurant calls. Maggots inside deep fried shrimp placed in front of customers. Rat chase through middle of busy restaurant. Mouse drinking from soda fountain spout (I've got a picture of it, somewhere....)

One of the weirdest calls I had was to a restaurant where one of the customers had been eating and drinking at a table on the second floor, by a window. The guy had apparently leaned back on his chair a little too far and fell out the window. The guy went through a small canopy, which slowed him down a bit, but it was still quite a ways down to the stone walkway. The windows were tall and attached at the middle on a fulcrum. And thus he went through sort of an ejector effect. If you pushed or fell on the bottom of the window too far, the other side (the top) would come (as I'm sure it did) whizzing around and smack you on your butt on the way out. It seems real tragic, but the thing was, even over and above the guy's being really understandably pissy to us (after falling out a window!)I mean I think falling out a window pretty much warrants being a little pissed off, right? Anyway, after we ship the guy off (in an ambulance) all these witnesses, not just restaurant people but people in his party, came forward, saying that the guy came in drunk, was being boisterous and belligerent. Someone even told him not to lean back on his chair!

We're, like, hey! the guy's his own worst enemy!

5. Halloween

I remember working a Halloween night one time that happened to fall on a Saturday night and coincided with the full moon. We knew it would be a busy night, because full moon nights always seemed to bring the crazies out of the woodwork (see **full moon theory of inner city mortality**). And the fact that it was Halloween put them in costumes and added another dimension of weirdness and excitement to the mix. Sure enough, we had plenty of fight calls, strange situations and disturbances during the evening. There were lots of people dressed up in costumes, joking around, bar-hopping and such. We had several calls about a guy wearing a "Jason" goalie mask and threatening people with a large knife or sword.

Some people seem to think that Halloween temporarily invalidates existing weapon laws. So you'll get guys dressed up like a samurai, walking around in public with live swords or ninja-wannabees twirling nunchaka or whipping "throwing stars" into dartboards at corner bars and the like. Of course, the more drinks these guys get in them, the more dangerous these situations become. Sometimes these guys start thinking they really are a samurai or whatever. It can get real ugly.

Anyway, we kept looking for this guy who was sending up red flags all over the place. He was a tall white male with short dark hair dressed in dark clothing, wearing a mask, and carrying a large sickle-like knife. Apparently he was walking up to people, brandishing the weapon, staring at people, not saying a word. This was upsetting many folks.

Finally one of our officers ran into him and attempted to question him. The guy pulled the same stunt he had been doing with civilians: he stayed in character and remained silent. The officer was trying to determine whether the sword was real or fake, but could not. Another disturbance broke out nearby, and the officer had to respond to that and break contact with the suspect. After we broke up the fight, we went looking for the "Jason" guy again, but couldn't find him. But we sort of knew we hadn't seen the last of him. As the night wore on and the bars let out for the night, we got a call of a disturbance involving 5-6 males and our "Jason" character in front of our of the local bars. When we arrived, we found the guy surrounded by a group of drunk males who were pissed off. He was using his sword-like weapon to keep them at bay. As we approached, the group dispersed when we told them we'd take care of the guy. We treated it like a felony stop, and once we got the weapon from him, we discovered that it was plastic, though it sure looked real, especially in the dark. We sent him packing. The guys he'd been messing with were intrigued when they found out the weapon was fake. We hoped the guy was as good at running as he was at scaring people.

6. "That's for making me run…."

One time my partner Ed and I were walking along Chatham Street in Boston, when we saw a kid come bolting around the corner running full tilt. It drew our attention 'cause the kid was running like someone was chasing him, not like he was out for a jog. He was running east, straight towards us….And sure enough, a few seconds later, a slightly overweight Boston police officer came huffing and puffing around the corner running after him. We cornered the kid and grabbed him for the BPD officer, who was still humping it up the street, towards us, with his nightstick in one hand (often you'll see officers carrying their nightsticks, when in foot chases, because it's hard to run with a nightstick on your belt.)

But as the officer reached us and the rabbit we'd caught, without breaking stride, he hauled off and smacked the kid with his nightstick, saying, "That's for making me run.." We both let go of the kid, shocked and feeling guilty that we'd even stopped him. It wasn't just that we'd inadvertently assisted an instance of police brutality, but what the cop said made it worse. I mean if the kid had just kicked him in the balls or something … that might be different but…

—Aaron

APPENDIX III

The ABCs of Poteet Cop Talk Quiz
or
Take the Poteet Cop Talk Quiz

Phrase   A N S W E R   *Authors' comments or hint*

1. **airmail**_____"Right up there with mailbox base-ball, for some kids!"

2. the **best cop money can buy**_____"I'm by the book, sarge, honest, clean as a whistle.!" "Yeah, sure, O'Malley, you're the best cop money can buy."

3. **CYA**_____"If not, good luck, amigo!"

4. got a **divorce**_____"Shut up and piss in your boot, like you always do when we're on stakeout."—thanks, Gilbert Shelton

5. **eyefuck**_____"Not as gross as it sounds."

6. **fag factory**_____"Not a pretty picture!"

BONUS Question: **fecal gravity**_____"We get the picture!"

7. **Go ahead, make my day**_____"You put it so well, Harry, my man."

141

8.   the old **Habeas Grabbus**_____"Enjoy your work much, do you there officer?"
Bonus Question: **helping a case**_____"What's a little perjury between friends?"
Bonus Question: **hinky**_____"A man runs out of a sorority house."

9.   **inching**_____"Ouchie!"

10. **jumping in**_____"Brotherly love at its finest."

11. **kicking ass and taking names**_____"Some of them are tattooed on that way."
liquid courage_____"What are you staring at, dickhead?"
Bonus Question: **lollipop gangsters** _____"See **Club Fed**, 'what's this with the pussification of America's crime world?'"—thanks, George Carlin.

13. **maggot   farm**_____"Hey!   who   picked these….?"
Bonus Question: **member of the deer family** _____"This is an easy one! Here's a hint: 'Doe, a deer. a female deer.'"

14. **a New York minute**_____"Not very long at all, closer to a second."

15. **Old Sparky**_____"What's that smell?"

16. **pop**_____3   correct   answers (drug lingo, cop talk, organized crime)

17. **quick change scam**_____"Wanna buy a bridge?"

18. **righteous shooting**_____"The victim was a lawyer, just kidding!"

19. **squirrel sheriff**_____

20. **throwdown**_____
uniform_____"Sitting duck."
vampires_____

23. **war story**_____"Let me tell you about the time...."

Bonus Question: **wood shampoo**_____"Not balsam wood shampoo."

24. **xerox machine polygraph ploy**_____"Does it have anything to do with sitting on the photocopier and making copies of your BUTT?"

25. **you're on your own**_____"My former bosses favorite expression."

26. **zing**_____"You got me!"

Award yourself 2 points for each answer you get even remotely close to our books definition. Add 1 point for any answer you give which while not necessarily right, is imaginative or amusing. Wit and charm will get you a long way in this world!

0–10	don't go outside after dark without an escort
10–20	perhaps a desk job would suit you better
20–30	patrolman
30–40	sergeant
40–50	SWAT
50–60	ace detective or master criminal

from—-Aaron C. and Lewis J. Poteet's **COP TALK,** forthcoming from iUniverse.com

ABOUT THE AUTHOR

Authors Lewis J. Poteet and Aaron C. Poteet, father and son, also wrote *Hockey Talk*, a dictionary of hockey slang. This book was born out of the son's lifelong fascination with police, crime and justice, and his father's love of language. Lewis has written several slang word books including *Plane Talk, Car Talk and The South Shore Phrase Book*. Lewis taught English for 32 years at Concordia University in Montreal and in winter 2000, was adjunct instructor in English at Austin (TX) Community College. Aaron holds a bachelor's degree in criminal justice from Northeastern University in Boston. He has walked the city streets at night as neighborhood patrol, Guardian Angel, even vigilante. His obsession with the street led to work in the most thankless profession known to man--law enforcement, working as a Special Police Officer in Boston and then briefly with the Austin Police Department. He now works for a large corporation in field collections.

Printed in the United States
894900004B

9 780595 133758